MY BEST PUZZLES IN LOGIC AND REASONING

By HUBERT PHILLIPS
(*"Caliban"*)

DOVER PUBLICATIONS, INC.
NEW YORK

Published in Canada by General Publishing Company, Ltd., 30 Lesmill Road, Don Mills, Toronto, Ontario.
Published in the United Kingdom by Constable and Company, Ltd., 10 Orange Street, London WC 2.

My Best Puzzles in Logic and Reasoning, first published by Dover Publications, Inc., in 1961, is a new collection of puzzles by Hubert Phillips, selected from the periodicals indicated in the preface.

Standard Book Number: 486-20119-8
Library of Congress Catalog Card Number: 61-66253

Manufactured in the United States of America
Dover Publications, Inc.
180 Varick Street
New York, N. Y. 10014

PREFACE

This little book, which is complementary to *My Best Puzzles in Mathematics*, contains puzzles which demand no mathematical knowledge, but which call for clear thinking and an ability to establish the logical relationships which the data presented imply. Some of them are quite simple; others—e.g., the "Colorful Isles" and such puzzles as "Tellham Nuthen"— are likely to baffle the beginner. But anyone who works his way through the book and is satisfied that he understands the solutions will, by the time he has finished, be able to tackle any similar problems undismayed.

The puzzles in this collection are of about thirty different types. I can fairly claim to be the "only begetter" of practically every one of them. Like *My Best Puzzles in Mathematics*, they were originally published serially in the *Daily Telegraph*, the *Evening Standard*, *Truth*, and the *Law Journal*.

London   HUBERT PHILLIPS
August, 1960

CONTENTS

Contents

Contents

PUZZLES

1 CATS AMONG THE PIGEONS

Messrs. Downs, Heath, Field, Forest, and Marsh—five elderly pigeon fanciers—were worried by the depredations of marauding cats owned by five not less elderly spinsters, and, hoping to get control of the cats, they married these ladies.

The scheme worked well for each of them so far as his own cat and pigeons were concerned; but it was not long before each cat had claimed a victim and each fancier had lost his favorite pigeon.

Mrs. Downs's cat killed the pigeon owned by the man who married the owner of the cat which killed Mr. Marsh's pigeon. Mr. Downs's pigeon was killed by Mrs. Heath's cat. Mr. Forest's pigeon was killed by the cat owned by the lady who married the man whose pigeon was killed by Mrs. Field's cat.

Who was the owner of the pigeon killed by Mrs. Forest's cat?

2 INVOCATION

Dr. Whackem assembled the eight prefects in his study.

"Well, boys," he said, "here we are again. Since it seems impossible to discover who released the mice in the laboratory, I propose to give seven of you a flogging. Lest, however, it be said that I do not temper justice with mercy, the eighth will go unscathed."

"And which of us is the eighth, sir?" asked Nosey.

"That," said the doctor, "I propose to leave to the arbitrament of chance. Let us seat ourselves at the table."

"In any order, sir?" asked Crayfish.

"In any order," said the doctor. "I propose—to adopt a phrase of Macbeth's—to push you one by one from your stools. The lad who lasts longest can laugh the loudest."

The boys were seated as follows. On the doctor's right, Crayfish. Next to him, Jay. Then Stingo, Nosey, Boor, Lollipop-Lollipop, Widdershins; and Foolardy on the doctor's left.

"What happens now, sir?" asked Boor. "An invocation to call fools into a circle?"

"Ha; very good, Boor," said the doctor. "What we want, however, is an invocation to call fools out of one. Yours will serve as well as any other. A pity, though, that under its operation you become Public Victim Number One."

Which boy escaped flogging?

3 MR. YELLOW

You may recall that, on Citrus Island, three tribes—the Whites, the Oranges, and the Lemons—have different standards of veracity. (They are otherwise indistinguishable.) Whites always tell the truth; Oranges always lie; Lemons, when asked a series of questions, tell the truth and lie alternately. A Lemon's first answer in a series may be either true or otherwise.

A visitor was somewhat confused recently when he was introduced to three natives named White, Orange, and Lemon, who are—not necessarily respectively—a White, an Orange, and a Lemon. There was also a fourth native named Yellow. The visitor asked each of the first three natives (a) what his own tribe was, and (b) what was Mr. Yellow's tribe.

To these questions, Mr. White replied: "I'm not a White. Mr. Yellow is an Orange."

Mr. Orange replied: "I'm not Orange. Mr. Yellow is a Lemon."

Mr. Lemon replied: "I'm not Lemon. Mr. Yellow is a White."

To which tribe does Mr. Yellow actually belong?

4 FIVE CANDIDATES

Five candidates—Ainsworth, Borrow, Coleridge, Defoe, and Emerson—competed for the President's Medal at All Saints. There were also five subjects: English, History, Latin, Greek, and Philosophy.

Marking was on an "ordinal" basis. The candidate placed first in a subject secured five marks; the candidate placed second, four marks; the remaining candidates, three, two and one marks respectively. Final placings depended on the aggregate marks scored.

No two candidates tied in any subject.

Ainsworth won the medal easily, with the excellent aggregate of 24 marks. Coleridge showed consistency: he secured the same mark in each of four subjects. Emerson took first place in Greek and third place in Philosophy.

No two candidates secured the same aggregate of marks, their final placing corresponding, as it happened, to the alphabetical order of their names.

How many marks did Borrow secure in Greek?

5 EXCHANGE OF AMENITIES

"Would you like some material for a puzzle?" asked a friend whom I met at the club.

"Certainly."

"It concerns five friends of mine. For the purposes of the puzzle I propose to call them Mr. Ham, Mr. Whisky, Mr. Goose, Mr. Sherry, and Mr. Port. Each of them, last Christmas, sent a present to one of the others. No two sent the same present. And of each present one of the five gentlemen concerned was the (pseudonymous) namesake; though none either dispatched or received the present corresponding to his own name. All clear so far?"

"Perfectly, thank you."

"Good," said my friend. "Now for what you call the data. Mr. Ham sent sherry to Mr. Port. The recipient of the port sent a goose to Mr. Ham. The namesake of the present dispatched by Mr. Sherry sent his own gift to Mr. Goose."

"And I have to deduce what each of them sent and received?"

"No," said my friend. "There are insufficient data for that. All you have to discover is the donor of the gift received by Mr. Sherry."

What is the answer?

6 ACCOMPLISHMENTS

"My four granddaughters are all accomplished girls." Canon Chasuble was speaking with evident self-satisfaction. "Each of them," he went on, "plays a different musical instrument and each speaks one European language as well as— if not better than—a native."

"What does Mary play?" asked someone.

"The cello."

"Who plays the violin?"

"D'you know," said Chasuble, "I've temporarily forgotten. *Anno Domini*, alas! But I know it's the girl who speaks French."

The remainder of the facts which I elicited were of a somewhat negative character. I learned that the organist is not Valerie; that the girl who speaks German is not Lorna; and that Mary knows no Italian. Anthea doesn't play the violin; nor is she the girl who speaks Spanish. Valerie knows no French; Lorna doesn't play the harp; and the organist can't speak Italian.

What are Valerie's accomplishments?

7 YACHTS

Messrs. Spinnaker, Buoy, Luff, Gybe, and Windward are yacht owners. Each has a daughter, and each has named his yacht after the daughter of one of the others.

Mr. Spinnaker's yacht, the *Iris*, is named after Mr. Buoy's daughter. Mr. Buoy's own yacht is the *Daffodil*; Mr. Windward's yacht is the *Jonquil*; Mr. Gybe's, the *Anthea*.

Daffodil is the daughter of the owner of the yacht which is named after Mr. Luff's daughter. Mr. Windward's daughter is named Lalage.

Who is Jonquil's father?

8 THE FACETIOUS FANCIERS

It would be fun, thought seven facetious fanciers, to enter pseudonymically for the Crab's Bay Fur and Feather Show.

Each won first prize in a class of which one of the other six was the pseudonymous namesake.

The namesake of the exhibit for which Mr. Rabbit won first prize is married to a girl who was, curiously, a Miss Rabbit.

The fancier who won first prize in the Dog class is the husband of Mr. Pigeon's wife's sister.

The winning Rabbit was bred by its exhibitor's fiancée. (She was not a Miss Rabbit.)

The pseudonymous namesake of Mr. Dog's exhibit exhibited the Duck.

The namesake of the fancier who exhibited the Guinea Pig was exhibited by the pseudonymous namesake of Mr. Rabbit's exhibit.

Of the seven fanciers, only two are unmarried: Mr. Duck and Mr. Canary.

Messrs. Duck, Pigeon, and Guinea Pig all competed unsuc-
cessfully in the three classes of which they were the pseudonymous namesakes.

These facts have been assembled for me by one of the party,
who exhibited under the name of Mr. Cat. No one, by the way,
exhibited in a class in which he failed to win first prize.

In what class did each of the seven win his prize?

9 THE FORTY-NINE CLUB

The Forty-Nine Club was formed last year. Our not un-
ambitious aim is:

"To mold this sorry scheme of things entire."

Each of its members has a "code number." The code
numbers are not consecutive, but are devised *ad hoc*—by "the
integration of three relevant components." My friend Probe, for
example, is No. 110; Dr. Calico, the Assyriologist, is No. 98;
Mrs. Thwackstraw, inventor of cosmic psychiatry, is No. 207.
These data were offered me when I accepted the club's invita-
tion to join. "But before we induct you, Caliban," said the
President, "I must point out that we propose to spell your name
Kaliban."

What is my code number?

10 PLATYPUS

The members of the Private Zoo Associatic ᴸ (incorporating
the Animal Exchange Club) arranged last Christmas for an
"all-round swap" of surplus specimens. Five enthusiasts took
part in this deal: Mr. Zebra; Dr. Giraffe; Lady Platypus;
Colonel Tiger; and Sir Matthew Manatee. Each sent to one of

the others one of the animals of which these five worthies are the namesakes, and the "swap" was so arranged that each of the five was the recipient of one addition to his (or her) zoo. No one either sent, or received, the animal which is his own namesake. For example, it was not Lady Platypus who received a Platypus. Incidentally (and this fact may be useful) it wasn't the recipient of the Platypus who dispatched a Manatee.

Dr. Giraffe sent a Tiger to Sir Matthew Manatee. The namesake of the beast received by Lady Platypus sent a Manatee to the namesake of the beast which Lady Platypus dispatched.

Who did send a Platypus, and to whom?

11 A FESTIVE CHRISTMAS

Four young couples—the Browns, the Greens, the Whites, and the Pinks—are spending Christmas at a hotel on the South Coast. They did the same thing last year. They then arranged that every evening they should "reorganize" themselves for the purposes of the hotel dance—each husband being partnered for the evening by the wife of one of the others, while on two evenings the same combination of partnerships occurred. "A very successful idea it was, too," Mrs. Brown told me. "We stayed just long enough to exhaust every combination. I expect we shall do the same thing this year."

On the first evening Pink was partnered by Mrs. Green; on the third evening by Mrs. Brown; on the fourth evening by Mrs. White. Brown's partners were Mrs. Pink on the first evening and on the fourth; on the last three evenings his partners were Mrs. White, Mrs. Green, and Mrs. White. White paired off with Mrs. Pink on the third evening and on the seventh. On the final evening his partner was Mrs. Green. Green escorted Mrs. Pink on the second and penultimate evenings. On the fifth evening his partner was Mrs. White.

Who was Green's partner on the sixth evening?

12 CARNIVORES AT PLAY

The Lions, Tigers, Wolves, and Leopards are four "soccer" teams, amongst whom competition is very keen. They recently staged a small "league" contest, in which each team played one match against each of the others. In this contest the order of the four teams, as measured by the total number of goals scored, was (1) Lions; (2) Tigers; (3) Wolves; (4) Leopards.

The Lions won their match against the Tigers by 4 goals to 1. The Leopards won against the Wolves. The other four games were drawn.

What was the score in the match between the Wolves and the Leopards; and which team had the smallest number of goals scored against it?

13 BERRIES ISLAND

Berries Island is another island of the group in which differing standards of veracity are maintained by different tribes. The Blacks, Logans, and Rasps are not distinguishable save in this important respect. The Blacks always speak the truth; the Rasps, never; while the Logans speak the truth and lie alternately.

On a recent visit I was taken around by two guides, each of whom asserted that the other was a Logan; but whether either of these statements was true I had, at the time, no means of telling. We called first at the local Sports Club to witness the final throws for the Javelin Cup. The three finalists were said by one guide to be (in the order of their throws) a Black, a Logan, and a Rasp; but by the other to be a Rasp, a Black, and a Logan.

To which tribes did the two guides and the three finalists actually belong?

14 CELIA'S SIMPLE CIPHER

"Miss Georgina Padgham, Celia's form mistress, is away, ill."
wrote the Head to Celia's father. "Miss Auburn Head has
been taking her place. And I'm sorry to say that Celia dis-
rupted this morning's lessons by passing a message in code
around the class. None of us can decipher it, and Celia has,
in my view, aggravated her offense by informing Miss Head
that 'any idiot ought to be able to read it.' "

Can you decode Celia's message? Dr. Tranter (Celia's
father) deciphered it in five minutes:

```
T R A N T   E R B A N   T E R B I   P P E X T
O X P B E   R E N A I   J A L H A   N J H O X
P B N O B   H Q E S S   P E R O X   P J Y O J
E H Q Y U   Y R N J Y   O X G S R   H H M A D
E H X A Q   P E H V Y   O N T R P   D U T E X
T R N X A   D R X P H
```

15 MNEMONIC

Here is a simple mnemonic which has on occasion been used
as an intelligence test in English schools:

OTTFFSS...

What are the next three letters?

16 TOURNAMENT

Five bridge players arranged a private tournament; each
pair was to play one rubber against each of the three pairs

formed from the other players. As some were more "choosy" about seats than others, the following rules were agreed to:

(1) Colonel Curry would always sit West.

(2) Subject to Rule (1), Mr. Exit would always sit South.

(3) Subject to Rule (1), Dr. Axiom would always sit North or, when the North chair was occupied, East.

(4) Subject, again, to the priority of the above rules, Mr. Bogus would sit, whenever possible, on the left of Dr. Axiom; failing that, to the left of Mr. Exit.

"What a lot of nonsense," said Professor Dithering.

The N–S seats were the "lucky" ones. Only one rubber was won by E–W. On this occasion Axiom and Bogus were partners against Curry and Dithering.

What was the largest number of rubbers won by any one player?

17 BEAUTY CONTEST

Acorn, Blackbird, Colchicum, and Dude dined together the other night. Each has one rather pretty daughter. As the four diners sat over their port, someone started an argument about which of these girls would win a beauty contest.

"We'll vote on it," said Acorn. "I've thought up some rules which will give all the girls a chance. Each of us has five votes. He must use them all, and can distribute them how he likes, except that he mustn't give more than three to one girl. We'll each put a dollar in the kitty, and the girl with most votes gets the lot."

Acorn's plan was generally approved; ballot papers were distributed and the diners proceeded to vote. None "partitioned" his five votes in the same way as any of the others. Blackbird thought it a sound plan to treat his three friends' daughters all alike. Dude gave the maximum permissible vote to his own daughter Diana; Colchicum, who thought his daughter Candida conceited enough already, voted for the other three girls. Acorn gave the same vote to Candida as to her rival Blondie Blackbird. All this effort was wasted, however, as each girl secured five votes.

What support was accorded to Adela Acorn?

18 YACHTING GIRLS

"We're all keen on yachting in these parts," said my tow-headed friend, Thalia Collingwood. "Father has a yacht, and so has each of his four friends: Colonel Drake; Mr. Nelson; Sir Barnacle Hood; and Dr. Benbow.

"What's more, each of the five has just the one daughter, and each has named his yacht after the daughter of one of the others. So you see" (she concluded proudly) "there's a dear little yacht named after me."

Sir Barnacle's yacht is the *Gabrielle*; Mr. Collingwood owns the *Lorna*; Mr. Nelson, the *Rosalind*. The *Melissa*, owned by Colonel Drake, is named after Sir Barnacle's daughter. Gabrielle's father owns the yacht which is named after Dr. Benbow's daughter.

Who is Lorna's father?

19 BRACELETS

Miss Tryon is the teacher of a large class of girls at one of our more enterprising schools. She is responsible for several subjects, including what is vaguely called "handwork," but her principal interest is in mathematics.

"I tried an interesting experiment this week," she told me. "I had available a large number of beads. They were of three colors: red, yellow, and green.

"I showed my girls how to make seven-bead bracelets—the beads are just strung on threads at regular intervals—and then

I suggested that each girl should make a bracelet for herself. My only condition was that she should use three beads of any one color; two of a second color; two of a third."

"And what was the experiment exactly?" I asked.

"Why," said Miss Tryon, "I wanted to see how many different bracelets were produced by these haphazard instructions. There were thirty-two, which is about what might have been expected. It would have been possible—but only just possible—for every girl to construct a bracelet different in appearance from all the others."

How many girls are there in the class?

20 A NOVEL CHAMPION-SHIP

Granger, Webbe, Tivey, and Prickles—competitors in our club billiards championship—decided to run it on an altogether novel basis. Each was to play one game against each of the others. "If we score a point for each game won," said Granger, "there'll quite probably be a tie. I've a better plan. Let each of us score a point for each game won by any player whom he beats. Those points determine the championship. And it is not likely that there will be a tie."

Granger's plan was adopted. He began badly by losing to Prickles. Nevertheless he won the championship, while Tivey took the "wooden spoon."

What were the result of Webbe's three games?

21 WONDERFUL

"You're good at ciphers, aren't you, Dad?" said Peggy. "I've solved a few in my time," said her father.

"Have a stab at this one." On a half-sheet of paper Peggy had printed:

IMPS ELUDE
NEWS-RIME
—NERO

"It doesn't seem to make much sense," said Peggy's father. "What's the big idea?"

"Transliteration," said Peggy.

"Absurd, my good girl. There's not nearly enough material."

"I knew you'd say that," said Peggy, grinning. "Have a go, all the same. It has been described as too wonderful."

Can you—with the aid of this hint—transliterate Peggy's cipher?

22 UPPANDOWNE

In the hamlet of Uppandowne, in Doomshire, everyone belongs to one of two families. These are the Upwrights and the Downwrights. There is nothing especially distinctive about the members of either family, except that, if questioned, Upwrights always tell the truth and Downwrights always lie.

When I last visited Uppandowne I dropped in for a pint at the local hostelry. There were six villagers in the bar. Having ordered a round of drinks, I asked them, one after the other, how many of them were Upwrights. The first five answers I received were:

"Two of us are Upwrights."

"No; one of us."

"None of us is an Upwright."

"There are three of us."

"Yes; that's right, three."

Thus far, clearly it was impossible for me to tell how many Upwrights were present. The sixth villager's answer, however, solved the problem "beyond a peradventure."

How many Upwrights were there?

23 ALBERT'S UMBRELLA

"It was no mean dinner we had last Saturday," said Edward. "There were just the five of us: Albert, Brian, Charlie, Donald, and me. We mixed our drinks a little too freely, and what do you think the result was? Each of us went away with the hat belonging to one of the others; gloves belonging to another of them; an umbrella belonging to a third. It's taken us several days to sort them out.

"For example, the bloke who had my umbrella was under the impression that he also had Donald's hat. Then, after a lot of telephoning, he found that he was wrong about that."

Amused by this contretemps, I collected a few more clues. Brian took the hat of the diner who carried off Charlie's gloves. The owner of the gloves which Charlie took went off with Donald's umbrella. Donald himself took the umbrella whose owner's hat was worn by Albert. And the diner who took Brian's umbrella also took Albert's hat.

Who went home with Albert's umbrella?

24 BOOKS

Mr. Reader's five daughters each gave books for Christmas to one or more of her sisters.

Each presented four books, and each received four books; but no two girls allocated her books in the same way—e.g., only one gave two books to one sister and two to another. Bessie gave all her books to Alice; Cissie gave three to Edith.

Who were the donors of the four books received by Deborah?

25 STAFF CONFERENCE

Mr. Peddant, head of a newly organized secondary school, assembled his staff of teachers for their first weekly conference. Their names (believe it or not) were Algebra, Botany, English,

French, and History; and each was to be responsible for the subject of which one of the others is the namesake.

Unfortunately, Peddant had failed to make clear to his colleagues who was going to teach what. Each master, naturally, knew what it was that he had himself been engaged to teach, but he misidentified the subject of every one of the others. For example, Mr. Algebra was under the impression that Mr. Botany was to teach history, that Mr. History was to teach English, and that Mr. French was to teach French.

Also, rather oddly, no two masters attributed the same subject to any one of their colleagues. No wonder the conference was (as Mr. Algebra put it) "a masterpiece of muddle and misunderstanding."

Mr. Botany thought that the English master taught botany. Mr. History thought that the English master taught history. Mr. History thought that Mr. English taught French.

What subject did the English master think the Algebra master taught?

26 DRAKE GOES WEST

"How did Drake get on," I asked, "in the Plymouth Hoe Bowling Tourney?"

"Not at all well," said Raleigh. "In fact, he was bottom of his section."

"What, the players were divided into sections, were they?"

"Into two sections," said Raleigh. "Seniors and Juniors. That enabled us to complete the tourney in nine days. Each competitor played three games against each of the others in his section. Nine games in all on each of the nine days."

How many competitors were there in all?

27 BUNS

"Now for some buns, boys," said young Mr. Gallowglass, Sports Master (and also Maths Master) at the Treatemwell

Preparatory School. He was addressing the members of the First XI, who had just brought off a handsome win against Diddleham.

"How much each can we spend, sir?" asked someone.

Mr. Gallowglass named a suitable sum. "Let me see," he went on. "Buns at this shop cost 2, 3, 4, or 6 cents each. Each of you must lay out his money differently."

"It can't be done, sir," said Beetle, the School wicket keeper.

"Oh, yes it can," said Gallowglass. "It can just be done. And, by the way, here's another 30 cents, Beetle. With that you can buy me five 6-cent buns as a tactical reserve."

Forty-eight buns in all were purchased.

How much was each boy allowed to spend on himself?

28 BATTLE OF WITS

John and Mary were playing at Patball, an outdoor game of their own invention. In skill, there was nothing to choose between them.

They were playing to 21 points.

Mary had the sun in her face. "Look here, John," she said, "with the sun where it is now you're scoring about three points to my one. I ought to have a handicap."

"Okay," said John. "Or why not change over at half time? Say, when I've scored 10 points."

"Right," said Mary. She considered. "After all, John, you did win the toss. Let's change over when you've scored 12."

"A generous offer," said John. "I'll accept it, all the same."

What should be the result of the game?

29 TEN STATELY TREES

In the municipal park at Clodbury are to be seen ten stately trees. There are two ash trees, two sycamores, two beeches, two oaks, and two firs. They were planted to commemorate

Queen Victoria's coronation by five pretty girls from the neighborhood: Alicia Ash, Susan Sycamore, Belinda Beech, Olivia Oak, and the once famous Felicia ("Muffins") Fir.

Each girl planted two different trees; none planted a tree of which she is the namesake. This "elegant interchange of female courtesies" was devised by the Town Clerk.

The namesakes of the two trees planted by Miss Olivia both planted sycamores. The namesakes of the trees which "Muffins" planted both planted ash trees. Alicia Ash planted one beech tree and one sycamore.

What trees were planted by Belinda Beech?

30 PICKLED WALNUTS

Here is one of those exercises in inference, which so much appealed to Lewis Carroll. You are given a series of statements which may seem to you more or less absurd. But, on the assumption that these statements are factually correct, **what conclusion (if any) can be drawn?**

(1) Pickled walnuts are always provided at Professor Piltdown's parties.

(2) No animal that does not prefer Beethoven to Mozart ever takes a taxi in Bond Street.

(3) All armadillos can speak the Basque dialect.

(4) No animal can be registered as a philatelist who does not carry a collapsible umbrella.

(5) Any animal that can speak Basque is eligible for the Tintinnabulum Club.

(6) Only animals that are registered philatelists are invited to Professor Piltdown's parties.

(7) All animals eligible for the Tintinnabulum Club prefer Mozart to Beethoven.

(8) The only animals that enjoy pickled walnuts are those who get them at Professor Piltdown's.

(9) Only animals that take taxis in Bond Street carry collapsible umbrellas.

31 DIGITS ARE SYMBOLS

"Digits, girls, are only symbols," said Miss Piminy to her class. "We could use other symbols instead. Suppose, for example, that S E is the square of E. Then S T E T might also represent a perfect square."

"I don't see that, Miss Piminy," said Troublesome Tess, the *enfant terrible* of the class.

"Don't you, Tess? Then use your wits," said Miss Piminy. "Your comment" (she added) "gives me an idea." She wrote on the board:

$$S E E$$
$$T E S S$$
$$\overline{}$$

$$.\quad.\quad.\quad.$$
$$\overline{}$$

"There's an addition sum, girls, S, E, and T have the values mentioned already. What's the answer to my sum?—in my own notation, of course."

How quickly can you produce the answer?

32 ALLSPORTS

I went to tea yesterday with an old friend, Mrs. Allsports. She has three daughters: Amelia, Bella, and Celia. On the doorstep I met another friend, who remarked that her own daughter was spending a yachting holiday at Sandville with one of Mrs. Allsports's girls.

Over the teacups it turned out that all three of the daughters are on holiday. Their interests are diversified. One is at Mudville; one at Rockville; one at Sandville. To make the thing more confusing, one is playing tennis, one is yachting, and one is playing golf.

It further transpired that Amelia is not at Sandville, that Celia is not at Mudville, and that the girl who plays golf is not at Rockville. I tried to discover who the yachting enthusiast is but could only find out that she is not Celia.

Who is playing golf, and where?

33 PINK, WHITE, AND BLUE

You may recall that colorful island where there are three races, indistinguishable save in respect of their attitude towards the truth. A Blue always answers a question truthfully; a White always lies; a Pink, answering two or more questions, tells the truth and lies alternately; his first answer, however, may be either truthful or otherwise.

A visitor to the islands approached a group of three natives, whose names were Mr. Pink, Mr. White, and Mr. Blue. One was known to be a Pink, one a White, one a Blue. Taking Mr. Pink aside, the visitor put some questions to him.

"Mr. Pink," he said, "are you the Pink, the White, or the Blue?"

"I am the Pink, sir."

"And Mr. White?"

"He is the White."

"So Mr. Blue is the Blue?"

"Obviously."

Is Mr. Blue the Blue? If not, what is he?

34 YACHTING AT NORMOUTH

"The yachting season is in full swing," writes my Normouth correspondent. "Last week was enlivened by a series of five races in which five well-known owners took part. Each sailed each of their five yachts in succession, taking the helm of his own yacht on the final day (Saturday).

"On Tuesday, Captain Yawl sailed *Vivandière*. *Atlantis* was successful on Wednesday, when Sir George Gatling sailed her, and again on Thursday, when she was sailed by Mr. Mainbrace. On this day (Thursday) Captain Yawl sailed *Mosquito*, and Mr. Narwhal sailed *Porpoise*. On Friday, Captain Yawl sailed *Candida*. On the Wednesday, by the way, Admiral Crabbe sailed Gatling's yacht, while Gatling himself put up a good show on Thursday in the yacht which—sailed by Mr. Mainbrace—won a very close race on Friday."

Can you state in what order the five yachts were sailed by Admiral Crabbe?

35 HOLIDAYS

"Here we are again—my family and I," writes Mr. Bexhill from Deal. "Don't try our intelligence too highly, will you?"

Mr. Bexhill is one of five schoolmasters—the others are Messrs. Angmering, Clacton, Deal, and Exmouth—each of whom, every August, lends his house to one of the others. Each of them lives in a resort which is the namesake of one of the others; no two of them live in the same resort. And none of them, this year, is spending his holiday in the resort of which he is the namesake.

Mr. Clacton and family are living in Mr. Exmouth's house. The Bexhill resident is at Exmouth. The namesake of the resort where Mr. Clacton is spending his holiday is spending his own holiday at Bexhill.

Where is Mr. Exmouth?

36 POKER

One night last week Messrs. Baker, Dyer, Farmer, Glover, and Hosier were playing poker at their club. Each of these gentlemen is the namesake of the vocation of one of the others.

The dyer was seated two paces to the left of Mr. Hosier.

The baker sat two places to Mr. Baker's right. The farmer sat to the left of Mr. Farmer; Mr Dyer, on the glover's right.
What is the name of the dyer?

37 TWENTY MARBLES

A bag contains 20 marbles. They are of three different colors. There are 8 blue ones, 7 red ones, and 5 green ones.

You are invited to close your eyes and draw the maximum number of marbles consistent with your leaving in the bag (1) at least four marbles of any one color, and (2) at least three marbles of any second color.
How many should you draw?

38 WHIST

At our club Messrs. Banker, Dentist, Apothecary, and Scrivener play the good old game of whist. They don't care for bridge.

Each of these gentlemen is the namesake of another's vocation.

Last night the apothecary partnered Mr. Apothecary; Mr. Banker's partner was the scrivener. On Mr. Scrivener's right sat the dentist.
Who sat on the banker's left?

39 THREE ISLANDERS

Here's another puzzle about those mysterious islanders, the Blues, Pinks, and Whites. The Blues (it will be recalled) invariably tell the truth; the Whites invariably lie; the Pinks, when asked more than one question, tell the truth and lie alternately. A Pink's first answer to a series of two or more questions may be either truthful or otherwise.

A Blue, a Pink, and a White named (not necessarily respectively) Mr. Blue, Mr. Pink, and Mr. White were seated at a circular table. I put to each of them these two questions, going round the table in a clockwise direction:

(1) "What is the name of your right-hand neighbor?"

(2) "What is the name of your left-hand neighbor?"

The answers I received were: From the first native addressed: (1) Mr. White; (2) Mr. Blue. From the second: (1) Mr. Pink; (2) Mr. White. From the third: (1) Mr. White; (2) Mr. Pink.

To what races do Messrs. Blue, White, and Pink respectively belong?

40 MIMULA

My niece Mimula is an imaginative kid. When I saw her last week she was drawing and coloring a map of an imaginary island, "Man Friday's Land." It was divided into a number of states: Yellowsands, Mango Cokernut, Turtle Beach, and a great many others of which I forget the names.

She was about to color each state with a flat wash and had mixed about a dozen colors. "Why so many colors?" I asked her. "You don't need them all, do you?" "I want to make sure," said Mimula, "that no state is the same color on the map as one with which it has a common frontier."

"Even so, you won't want all those colors," I replied.

What is, in fact, the maximum number of colors required to differentiate from its neighbors each one of a number of contiguous states?

41 MACBETH

When Messrs. Banquo, Macbeth, Macduff, Duncan, and Donalbain all accepted parts in an amateur production of *Macbeth*, complications became inevitable. They were heightened by the stage director's decision to give each of these gentlemen the role of which another one is the namesake. Nor was this all. At the last moment, the stage director (a temperamental chap named Siward) decided to change all the roles round; and, when the play was finally put on, none of our five Thespians played either the part of which he was the namesake, or the part which he had rehearsed.

For example, Macbeth was played by the namesake of the part rehearsed by Mr. Banquo. Macduff was played by the namesake of the part rehearsed by Mr. Donalbain. Mr. Macduff, who had rehearsed the part of Donalbain, played that of Banquo.

Who played the part rehearsed by Mr. Macbeth?

42 PIOUS CIRCLE

At one time I belonged to an organization called the Pious Circle. Its members were of both sexes. One of them, who had been engaged to another and had thought better of it, sent her as a parting gift a ring with this inscription:

FOR A GIRL I LOVED CONTRIVED;
BY NATURE TOUGH, HER HEART SURVIVED.

The message has an ulterior significance. **Can you guess what its significance is?**

43 FALSEHOODS

Messrs. Draper, Grocer, Baker, and Hatter are (appropriately enough) a draper, grocer, baker, and hatter. But none of them is the namesake of his own vocation.

When I tried to find out who is who, four statements were made to me: (1) "Mr. Draper is the hatter." (2) "Mr. Grocer is the draper." (3) "Mr. Baker is not the hatter." (4) "Mr. Hatter is not the baker." But clearly there was something wrong here, since Mr. Baker is not the baker.

I subsequently discovered that three of the four statements made to me are untrue.

Who is the grocer?

44 COMMENTATOR

The *Commentator*, that mighty organ of opinion, employs five powerful publicists. Their real names are Arnott, Brisk, Cellini, Dacres, and Ewart; and they write (not necessarily respectively) under the pseudonyms of "Alba," "Jove," "Magnus," "Prospero," and "Thunderer."

The identities of these publicists have been a well-kept secret. The editor of the *Commentator* was much amused recently, when he discovered that each of the five was mistaken as to the identity of each of the other four. Moreover, each of the four pseudonyms not used by each publicist was attributed to him by one of his colleagues. Yet no two publicists attributed the same pseudonym to any one writer.

Cellini, for instance, thought that Brisk was "Magnus," Dacres thought that Ewart was "Alba," and that Cellini was "Prospero." Brisk identified Dacres as "Prospero," while Arnott took Brisk himself to be "Jove" and Dacres to be "Magnus."

Can you now deduce each publicist's pseudonym?

45 POOTLE BEACH

Pootle Beach regatta was a very minor affair. There were four races, and the same four yachts entered for all of them. So their owners decided that each of them should sail a different yacht in each race.

In the first race Commander Twostraws sailed Mrs. Feeble's yacht. In the second race Mrs. Feeble sailed the Hon. Norbert Nohow's. Mr. Candlehoof won the third race, sailing his own yacht, *Meteor*. Candlehoof, in fact, won all four races—not surprising, perhaps; as he knows Pootle Bay intimately.

Firefly, the largest yacht, was sailed by Nohow in the second race, and by Twostraws in the fourth. In that race she finished second to *Swallow*.

Who owns *Vega*?

46 CECILIA'S CODE

"Another puzzle for you, Uncle Timothy," said my precocious niece Cecilia.

"Hand it over."

"I haven't written it down," said Cecilia. "I'll tell it you. It's very simple. If each digit is represented by a letter, and the product of A B and C D is E E E, what is the product of A B and D?"

"I don't know," I said. "It's anyone's guess."

"You can't do it?"

"There are several solutions."

"I thought you'd say that," said Cecilia. "I'll give you another clue. Subtract A B from the product of E and C D, and you get C C."

"That's better," I said. "You have now a unique solution."

What (in Cecilia's code) is the product of A B and D?

47 MR. ETCHER

Messrs. Draftsman, Etcher, Musician, and Sculptor are a draftsman, an etcher, a musician, and a sculptor. Of none, however, are the name and the vocation the same.

The draftsman is not the namesake of Mr. Musician's vocation. The etcher is neither Mr. Sculptor, nor the namesake of Mr. Etcher's vocation.

Can you say what Mr. Etcher's vocation is?

48 TELLHAM NUTHEN

We have had several puzzles about the Colorful Isles, where some races are always truthful, and others always lie. But a correspondent reminds me that, much nearer home, we have the little-known village of Tellham Nuthen. Here, as a result of protracted inbreeding, the inhabitants all have one of two surnames: they are either Washingtons or Longbows. And—true to their names—Washingtons always tell the truth, and Longbows always lie.

I visited Tellham Nuthen recently and encountered three villagers in the quaint old High Street, I said to the first of them: "Are you Washingtons or Longbows?" He replied: "We are all Longbows." The second villager said: "No, that isn't true; only two of us are Longbows." And the third said: "That isn't true, either."

Was the third speaker a Washington or a Longbow?

49 SIX DINNERS

Four friends who spent a week's holiday together dined at the same table for six nights. Their "chairman," Mr. Butcher, always occupied the same seat, but the occupancy of the other three seats was on no two nights the same. On Monday night, Mr. Glover had the hosier to his right and the glover to his left. On Tuesday, Mr. Butcher had the butcher to his left; the butcher's other neighbor was Mr. Glover. On Wednesday, Mr. Hosier had the hosier to his right and the butcher to his left; while on Thursday the draper sat between the glover (on his right) and Mr. Draper. On Friday, the draper was on Mr. Hosier's left.

Who, on Saturday, were seated, respectively, on Mr. Butcher's right and left?

50 PETS

Alec and Bob and Cyril and David are the cause of much confusion in our village. Each of them owns a cat named after one of the other three and a dog named after another of them. No two cats, and no two dogs, have the same name.

For example, David's dog and Cyril's cat are both namesakes of the owner of the cat Cyril. The namesake of Bob's cat is the owner of the cat whose namesake owns the dog Alec.

Who owns the dog David?

51 GREEN CROSSES

"The scholarship will be awarded," said the Head to the three candidates—Chuckles, Wombat, and Breeze—"to the winner in this little competition. I am going to chalk a cross, which will be either a green cross or a red cross, on the forehead of each one of you. I shall then ask each boy who can see a green cross to hold his hand up; and to take his hand down as soon as he can tell me what color his own cross is. He must, of course, be able to explain how his answer is arrived at. Kindly close your eyes for ten seconds." He chalked a green cross on all three foreheads. "Go!" All three hands shot up in the air; that of Chuckles was almost immediately lowered. "My cross is green, sir."

How did Chuckles know?

52 CIPHER

Here is a simple transliteration cipher. Each letter of the original (which is in English) is represented by another letter: thus, if L occurred in the original it would have been represented throughout by N.

The words have, of course, been regrouped in sets of five letters.

EKSCK	WFKEE	KSCEP
REZAE	PCXBC	AEZKF

Here's a useful clue: PRINCE. This is the coded variant of a word which would put you on the right track at once.

53 FOUR STATEMENTS

Messrs. Fireman, Guard, and Driver are (not necessarily respectively) the fireman, guard, and driver of one of our fastest expresses. Who is what? When I tried to find out, I was given these four "facts":

(1) Mr. Driver is not the guard.
(2) Mr. Fireman is not the driver.
(3) Mr. Driver is the driver.
(4) Mr. Fireman is not the guard.

It then transpired that, of the above four statements, only one is true.

Who is what?

54 THREE NATIVES

Here's another test (not a very easy one) about that peculiar island where there coexist the Blues (who always tell the truth), the Whites (who always lie), and the Pinks (who, when asked a series of questions, tell the truth and lie alternately). But don't forget that a Pink's first answer may be a lie.

To George, Edward, and William, three natives of the island, I put these three questions: (1) What is your left-hand neighbor? (2) What is your right-hand neighbor? (3) What are you?

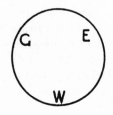

The three natives were seated as in the diagram, facing one another. Here are their answers:

George: (1) White,   (2) Pink,   (3) Blue.
Edward: (1) Pink,   (2) Pink,   (3) Blue.
William: (1) White,   (2) Blue,   (3) Blue.

To which race, in fact, does each of the three belong?

55 ZOO

"Can you square Z O O, Uncle Timothy?" asked my niece Celia.

"I beg your pardon?"

"I'll explain," said Celia. "This is one of those things where each letter stands for a digit. If you multiply Z O O by Z O O, you get T O P A Z."

"And you have to determine what the several digits are?"

"That's the idea," said Celia.

It's not very difficult.

How quickly can you (using Celia's notation) find the sum of TOP and PAT?

56 THREE HORSES

Antrobus, Daydream, Nevermore, and Witless each named his favorite horse after one of the others. To test the respective merits of these animals, they staged a race in which each rode one of the horses—neither his own, nor the one named after him.

Antrobus's horse was ridden by Nevermore; the horse Nevermore, by Witless. The horse Witless was ridden by the namesake of the horse ridden by Daydream.

What is the name of the horse that was ridden by the namesake of Antrobus's horse?

57 SCHOLARSHIP

I regret to report that five schoolgirls, who recently competed for a scholarship, decided that it would be "rather amusing" to send home mendacious—or partly mendacious—reports of the result.

Gay wrote: "I took second place. Joan was a little in front of Edwina." Edwina: "Gay was last. Mollie was well ahead of Pat." Joan: "I only took fourth place. Mollie came in second." Pat: "Joan was third. Edwina did better than Mollie." And Mollie: "Edwina took third place. Pat (to our surprise) won the scholarship."

No two candidates tied for a place. Each girl made one true statement and one false one.

In what order were the five candidates placed?

58 TALLYHO

At Tallyho College, the "seminary for young sportsmen," there are (as you may know) six houses. The Cricket Cup, for which the several houses compete during the summer term, is contested on a "league" basis: each of the six houses meets each of the others once. Three matches are played simultaneously on each of five successive Saturdays.

This summer the outstanding match on the first Saturday was between Quorn and Henley: Quorn won by three runs. On the second Saturday, Quorn defeated Wimbledon by an innings and 90 runs. On the third Saturday, Wimbledon, playing Belvoir, declared at 253 for no wicket. On the fourth Saturday, Lord's tied with Henley.

Which house played Twickenham on the fifth Saturday?

59 NAMESAKES

When those sprightly lads of our village—Joe Gladstone, "Slogger" Browning, "Tiny" Livingstone, Pete Tennyson, and

"Stuffy" Meredith—were invited to Lady Mackerel's fancy-dress dance, it seemed only fitting that each of them should go as the Eminent Namesake of one of the others. "Tiny" made a most impressive Mr. Gladstone; but "Slogger's" answer was in the negative when his hostess said to him: "Dr. Livingstone, I presume?"

The eminent namesake of the reveler who did, in fact, represent Dr. Livingstone was represented by the reveler whose eminent namesake was represented by Pete Tennyson. These three were all awarded prizes.

Can you say who—complete with false beard, slouch hat, and cloak—represented Queen Victoria's favorite poet?

60 THREE VILLAGERS

An earlier puzzle was concerned with the little-known village of Tellham Nuthen, where everyone's surname is either Washington or Longbow. The Washingtons (let me remind you) always tell the truth, and the Longbows, when you question them, always lie.

On my second visit to Tellham Nuthen, I once again met three villagers coming down the High Street. I stopped and ventured to inquire whether they were Washingtons or Longbows. The first villager replied: "Two of us are Washingtons." The second said: "Nonsense, only one of us is a Washington." The third said: "Yes, that is quite true."

What, in fact, were the surnames of the three villagers?

61 EQUESTRIAN

Catkin, Jorkin, Lambkin, and Pipkin each named his favorite horse after one of the other three. In a recent trial, each rode one of the four horses. None, however, rode either his own horse or the horse named after him.

Lambkin rode Catkin's horse. The horse owned by Pipkin was ridden by the namesake of Lambkin's horse. The owner of Catkin rode Pipkin.

Can you name the horse of which the rider of Lambkin is the owner?

62 AT RANDOM

A bag contains equal numbers of blue and red marbles. If two of them are drawn from the bag at random, the odds against their both being red are four to one.

Instead of drawing these two marbles, however, I draw (at random) some of the marbles from the bag, and transfer them to a second bag, which I will call Bag No. 2. Now one marble is drawn at random from Bag No. 1, and a second marble from Bag No. 2.

What are the odds against their both being blue?

63 DOMINANT FIFTH

"What's the Dominant Fifth?" asked Dr. Dingo, as his daughter Cicely came in from school.

Cicely blushed. "Just a secret society," she said. "I'm one of the vice-presidents."

"And you're meeting tonight; is that right?"

"How on earth did you know?" asked Cicely.

"You left this lying about. That's no way to keep secrets, my girl." He handed Cicely this paper:

DOMINANT FIFTH

REASM NCNVE OTMLE SEHST TAOEI

"How did you manage to read it?" asked Cicely. "The code is known to only about eight of us."

"Change it," said Dingo. "Any fool can read that."

This may be an exaggeration. But it's not a difficult code.

Can you decipher it?

64 "I'M A WASHINGTON"

You may recall that in the village of Tellham Nuthen everyone's surname is either Washington or Longbow. The Washingtons always tell the truth, the Longbows always tell lies.

Meeting a group of four villagers in the street, I put my customary inquiries as to whether they were Longbows or Washingtons. The first villager replied: "We are all Longbows." The second: "Only one of us is a Longbow." The third: "No; two of us are Longbows." The fourth: "I'm a Washington."

Now, a villager who says "I'm a Washington" may clearly be either a Washington or a Longbow.

Was the fourth speaker a Washington?

65 CASCA

Among my "horsy" acquaintances, five of the keenest are Armitage, Blood, Challenger, Dobbin, and Fox. Recently a race was staged in which five horses competed: Ajax, Briareus, Casca, Dolabella, and Fulmen. Each of my five friends had trained one of these animals, and rode another one; and I noted with interest that none had either trained or ridden a horse of which the name has the same initial letter as his own.

Armitage trained the horse ridden by Challenger; Dobbin, the horse ridden by Armitage. The name of Dolabella's rider has the same initial as the name of the horse ridden by Armitage; the name of Briareus's rider has the same initial as the name of the horse ridden by Blood.

Who trained the winning horse, Casca?

66 BUSES

On route 71X buses start from the Green Man at Ilworth and ply backwards and forwards between that hostelry and the Shabby Tiger at Plugstead. There are 11 buses on this route; each, on arriving at either terminus, waits for one minute and then begins the return journey.

Mr. Brightly, a bus driver from the provinces, boarded a bus at the Green Man the other day and rode all the way to the Shabby Tiger, making a note every time he passed a 71X bus. He passed one (so he calculated) every 1,320 yards, and estimated their average speed at 15 m.p.h.

How many buses did he pass en route?

67 BOREHAM

"Talking of birthdays," said Boreham at the club, "there have been some odd coincidences in my family."

"Really?" said Captain Stoney, who hoped to touch Boreham for a fiver.

"My great-great-grandfather, my great-grandfather, my grandfather, my father, I myself, and my son were all born on the thirteenth of the month," said Boreham. "And, what is more, in successive months. My great-great-grandfather in January; my great-grandfather in February; and so on."

"So your boy was born in June?" said Stoney intelligently.

"Correct," said Boreham. "And here's the second coincidence. The year in which my kid was born was the square of my then age in years. The year in which my father was born was the square of my grandfather's then age in years. And the year in which my great-grandfather was born was the square of my great-great-grandfather's then age in years. Amazing, don't you think so?"

"Fascinating," said Captain Stoney.

What was the date of birth of Boreham's great-great-grandfather?

68 CONFERENCE

"What a conference!" writes a friend who is one of these international busybodies. "There are six official languages (in addition to English): French, German, Spanish, Dutch, Polish, and Welsh. And someone with a perverted sense of humor has engaged six interpreters whose surnames are likewise French, German, Spanish, and so on.

"Each of these six chaps can speak two of the six languages, and each language is spoken by two of them. None speaks the language which corresponds to his own name."

Here, thought I, is material for a test. I find that Mr. French and Mr. Dutch account—between them—for the four languages of which neither is the namesake. Of the two languages spoken by Mr. Dutch, both the namesakes speak French. Mr. Spanish speaks Dutch and German; one of his colleagues speaks Dutch and Polish; none of the interpreters speaks both Polish and German.

What two languages does Mr. Polish speak?

69 TRANSLITERATE

Here is that simple, but always popular, exercise: a transliteration cipher. This is to say, each letter used in the original message is represented by the same letter throughout. Such messages are, of course, not difficult to decipher if there is a sufficiency of material.

In this case I have taken a well-known line from Shakespeare. The separate words are not shown, but the letters composing them have been regrouped in fives:

TAPSD	TOSXA	ETEMS	COSKP
MWSKO	BOQSA	WLTAP	SDTOS

How quickly can you decipher Shakespeare's message?

70 PENNY GREEN

"How do I get to Penny Green?"

"Take a train from the underground station, just round the corner."

"Any train?"

"No, some of the trains run to Shillingstone. But, more likely than not, the next will be a Penny Green train. In fact—let me see—the odds are about five to one in favor of it."

"I get you. There are very few trains to Shillingstone?"

"On the contrary. They run alternately with the trains to Penny Green."

"Then you must be familiar with the timetable. There's a five to one chance if I hurry."

"I shouldn't, old man. I know no more about the train times than I've told you."

They why does he say (I asked myself) that the odds are on a train to Penny Green?

71 CROSS CURRENTS

An unusual situation developed during the last election in the rural constituency of Cross Currents.

There were five candidates: a Socialist; a Tory; a Liberal; a Communist; and a Total Abstainer. The candidates' names were Mr. Dizzy; Mr. Fabian; Mr. Gladstone; Mr. Marx; and Mr. Pussyfoot. To make the thing more confusing, the daughter of each of these candidates (reacting, as daughters will, from parental guidance) acted as agent for one of the others. And none of the five candidates or of the five agents was associated with the platform naturally suggested by his or her name.

For example, the Socialist candidate was Mr. Dizzy, and the Communist agent was Freda Fabian. Dolores Dizzy acted as agent to Mr. Pussyfoot, while the Socialist agent was the Communist candidate's daughter.

What was the name of the Total Abstainer?

72 A FAIR COP

"What do you get if you multiply X X by itself?" my niece Cecilia asked me.

"C C C C," I replied. "Twenty times twenty is four hundred."

"Aha!" said Cecilia. "You're jumping to conclusions, Uncle Timothy. X X isn't 20; it's a code of my own, in which each digit is represented by a letter. And X X multiplied by itself is M M C C."

"I see," I said, rather stuffily. It was a "fair cop."

"Try again," said Cecilia. "Divide X X by C and square the quotient. What does it come to in my notation?"

Can you do that one?

73 SLITELY FONEY

"It may strain your credulity" (writes the headmaster of Slitely Foney) "to learn that in one of our forms are five boys named French, English, Science, German, and Algebra. It will certainly surprise you—and perhaps afford the basis of a test—when I tell you that these five boys, collectively, carried off the first, second, and third prizes in the subjects which correspond to their names. Each boy secured one first prize, one second, and one third. And I need hardly add that no boy was successful in a subject of which he is the namesake."

On making further inquiries, I found that the namesake of the subject for which German took first prize took, himself, first prize for English and second prize for Science. The namesake of the subject for which Algebra took second prize secured the first German prize, and the second prize for French. And the namesake of the subject for which French took second prize took the first prize for Algebra and the third prize for English.

Who secured the three French prizes?

74 MISS BRIGHTSANDS

"We made rather a hash of the election of Miss Brightsands," writes Bob. "I was one of the committee of seven, as you know, and we thought it would be fairest to allow those of us who were in two minds about the girls to split their votes if they wanted to. So each of us had five votes, which he could divide among the five candidates in any way he pleased. We were awfully ingenious about this—no two of us divided his votes in the same way—but the net result was that all the girls dead-heated. And we finally drew a name out of a hat."

I went into the question of the voting. George had "plumped" for his fiancée, Enid, while Harry gave four of his votes to Laura. John, on the other hand, voted for all the girls except Diana; and Dick, in an access of indecision, fatuously voted for them all. Cyril gave Mary and Diana one vote each; Bob also couldn't make up his mind between these two; John's favorite was Susan.

Where did the rest of Susan's votes come from; and how were Alec's votes distributed?

75 SANDRA

"Fancy meeting you!" I exclaimed. "You *are* the Cormorant, aren't you?"

We had been at Oxford together. The "Cormorant" was secretary of the Ghost Club the year that I was president. Neither of us had seen or heard anything of the other for nearly thirty years.

"And this little girl," I said. "Is she yours?"

"Indeed she is. I've been married for the last ten years."

"What's your name, my dear?" I asked.

"Sandra," she said shyly.

"Is it now? The same name as your mother's!"

How did I know that?

76 SURNAMES

Five close friends (all employed in the same business) are Messrs. Frank, George, James, Thomas, and Walter. (These are their surnames.) Each, as it happens, has two sons; and each thought it would be a pleasing fancy to give each of his sons, as his Christian name, the surname of one of his four friends. So the ten boys comprise two Franks, two Georges, two Jameses, two Thomases, and two Walters.

The namesake of Mr. Walter's two boys both named one son Frank. The namesake of Mr. James's two boys both named one son George. Neither of Mr. Frank's sons is a Walter.

What are the names of Mr. Thomas's boys?

77 NUMBER PLATES

Sam Carter, Edward Jones, Henry Patterson, and Roy Butcher had parked their cars side by side at the golf club. They were intrigued to notice that the license plates of their cars (not respectively) were:

S A M 2075	E D W 4534
H E N 8862	R O Y 6183

"It looks," said Sam Carter, "as though we should swap the plates round."

"Not a bit of it," said Roy Butcher, who had been studying them intently. "In one respect each owns the car which it is most appropriate he should have."

None of the others could find the clue to Roy's (perfectly correct) inference. Can you?

And, if so, which was Roy Butcher's car?

78 NINE DANCES

Alibi, Boron, Camomile, and Dunce took their wives to the Tennis Club dance. They danced nine dances, and, by general agreement, none of the four men danced any of them with his own wife. Moreover, the eight dancers paired off differently for each of the nine dances.

Is this possible? Certainly it is.

Alibi danced the first two dances with Mrs. Boron, and the next with fascinating Clare Camomile. For the fourth, fifth, and sixth dances, Boron's partner was Minnehaha Dunce. Dunce danced the seventh dance with his sister, Nectarine Alibi, and the eighth with Mrs. Camomile.

How were the eight dancers paired for the last dance?

79 THE RUMPUS CLUB

Mr. Daubwell, the portrait painter, was asked to paint the historic meeting at which Lord Rumple and Lord Crocus, and four of their relatives, founded the Rumpus Club. The six gentlemen in question had been dining at a circular table; they were all closely related and called one another by their Christian names.

Daubwell's problem was to discover, some time after the event, how the six diners were seated at the table.

Lord Crocus told him: "I sat two places to the left of Gilbert."

Lord Rumple's cousin said: "Herbert sat two places to my right. Lord Rumple was on Egbert's left, and Robert on Egbert's right."

Lord Rumple's brother said: "Albert was on my right; Lord Crocus's cousin, on my left."

Lord Crocus's brother said: "I sat directly opposite Herbert."

Ethelbert said: "I sat next but one to Robert."

Who is who? And how were the six diners seated?

80 REGATTA

Four yachts, competing in our local regatta, belong to four friends who are members of the same club: Admiral White, Mr. Brown, Captain Green, and Dr. Moon. Each yacht has been named by her owner after one of his three friends, and each is to be sailed by one of the four yachtsmen named: in no case either her owner or her namesake.

Admiral White does not own the yacht *Green*; Captain Green is not the owner of *Moon*. Dr. Moon is not sailing *Brown*. The general expectation is that the winning yacht will be either *Brown* or *Green*; but Admiral White thinks the vessel he is sailing should have the measure of both of them.

Who is going to sail Captain Green's yacht?

81 EPICENE

This summer four families were staying at the same hotel as I was. Each family consisted of father, mother, son, and daughter, and all the members of these families called one another by their Christian names. This was very confusing. One father was named Alison; one was named Jocelyn; one was named Hilary, and the fourth was named Sydney. Similarly, one mother, one son, and one daughter bore each of these four names. Moreover, no two members of a family had the same Christian name.

For example, Alison (the daughter) told me one morning that the young people were about to play tennis, while their parents had made up two tables at Canasta. She (Alison) and her fiancé, Jocelyn, were playing against Sydney's brother and Hilary, while the two Sydneys took on Hilary and his fiancée, Jocelyn. The Canasta games were mixed doubles also. The girl Alison's mother and Hilary had been challenged by the two Alisons, and Alison's fiancé's father was paired with Hilary against the two Jocelyns.

What was the name of Jocelyn's husband?

82 CISSIE'S PARTY

Five of her friends had tea with Cissie on the occasion of her twelfth birthday. They sat around the dining-room table, with the birthday-cake in the middle. How had they been seated? The question came up for discussion some weeks later, when—as it happened—all six girls were present.

Cissie said: "Evelyn was on my right." Evelyn said: "Frances was on my right." Betty said: "Antoinette was on my left." Frances said: "I was on Cissie's right." Antoinette said: "I had Doris on my right." Doris said: "I was on Betty's left."

Two of these statements were untrue.

How, in fact, were the six girls seated?

83 MIXED DOUBLES

Four young couples—the Greens, the Pinks, the Browns, and the Whites—are all keen table-tennis players. They have organized a mixed-doubles tournament which is to take place in the spring.

The conditions are that each husband will play one match in partnership with the wife of each of the others, against every similar partnership. In no case will a husband and wife play together. Two matches will be played on each evening set aside for the tournament.

How many evenings in all will the tournament occupy?

84 CROSSING THE BAR

"Have a stab at writing poetry," said "Nosey" Nooks, the English master, who was getting a trifle bored with his form. "Something on the lines of, say, 'Crossing the Bar'— that shouldn't be difficult. I'll give prizes of two model airplanes for the best poems handed in."

Jimmy James didn't want a model airplane and had no

intention of writing any poems. He amused himself by concoct-
ing a "code message" for his cronies. It ran as follows:

SYPAA	SKEYS	SAPEK	
APSYS	ASYEA	KEYSY	PYKE.
EYSSK.			

The key word ought to be obvious in more senses than one.
Can you deduce what Jimmy's key word is?

85 SIMPLE CIPHER

"The boys seem to be overexcited," said Mrs. Graymatter
to her husband, the Professor. "Too many parties, I suppose.
Can't you think up something to keep them quiet for a bit?"

"I suppose I could," said Graymatter.

After half an hour's cerebration he produced the following,
which he handed to his four obstreperous sons. "Have a go at
this," he said. "There'll be a prize of a dollar for the first
solution that makes sense."

SANTA BE AS SANT SUPS MOSU TYRTOS MAE.

"What is it?" asked young Joe. "A cipher?"

"Correct. A cipher of the simplest possible type."

An hour went by; there was no sign of a solution. "We're
stumped," said Jim. "Can't you give us some sort of clue?"

"If you really need one," said Graymatter. "Indeed, I'll be
generous: I'll give you two clues. The first is UPLITS; the second
is OAIMIAYRD. And the first gives utterance to the second."

Can you decode Graymatter's cryptogram?

86 IMPERFECT MEMORIES

"Here," said Dean Dodswell, "is an amusing example of
human fallibility.

"Four of my friends were playing bridge last week. A few
days later, when an argument arose, they tried to reconstruct
the position. They agreed that the four seats at table should be
called North, South, East, and West.

"Colonel Ratbane said: 'I was sitting South. My right-hand adversary was Mrs. Beetle.'

"Mrs. Beetle said: 'I sat East, Colonel Ratbane was on my right.'

"Dr. Whatknott said: 'I sat North. On my right was Mrs. Peewit.'

"And Mrs. Peewit said: 'I sat South. My right-hand opponent was Dr. Whatknott.' "

"And how, in fact, were they seated?" I asked.

"You can work that one out," said Dean Dodswell. "You'd get the answer without any difficulty if you knew how many statements were untrue."

How were the four players seated?

87 MUSICAL FLOP

"My musical party was a flop," writes the Dowager Lady Piccolo. "I'd invited four celebrities: a pianist, a cellist, a flutist, and an organist. None of them listened to my introductions; they all had so much to say. Crotchet, for example, got it into his head that Minim was the flutist. And similarly with the rest of them; each of the four misidentified the other three, though no two of them made the same misidentification. Thus the instrument which Quaver thought Breve played was assigned by Breve to Minim.

"Minim took Quaver to be the cellist. Quaver, idiotically, thought that Crotchet was the pianist, and so on. You might like to have a stab at working the rest out for yourself."

What instrument does Breve play; and what did he suppose was played by Crotchet?

88 SEVENTEEN MARBLES

A bag contains seventeen marbles. They are of four different colors: there are at least two of each color; and of no two colors are there the same number.

The color of which there is the largest number is green. If I draw from the bag enough marbles—but only just enough—to ensure that I have at least two of any one color, and at least one of any second color, I must draw eleven.

How many must I draw to ensure that at least one of the marbles drawn is a green one?

89 INTERHOUSE HOCKEY

The four houses at Miss Pinkerton's Academy bear the somewhat incongruous names of Boadicea, Godiva, Darling, and Nightingale. They compete against one another annually for the Interhouse Hockey Shield. Each house plays one game against each of the others, two points being awarded for a win and one point for a draw.

Scoring was high in last year's competition. No two games produced the same score, though the aggregate of goals scored was the same in every match. On a points basis, the order of finishing was: (1) Darling (winners of the Shield); (2) Godiva; (3) Nightingale; (4) Boadicea.

Darling scored eight goals more than were scored against them. Nightingale scored 15 goals and 15 goals were scored against them. Boadicea clocked up three goals in one game, all of which were penalties.

What was the result of the game between Darling and Nightingale?

90 PROSPECTIVE GRADUATES

Dr. Wiseman has one son at each of three universities; Manchester, Nottingham, and Reading. They are all reading different subjects, which you will find mentioned below.

John, the eldest, is not at Manchester. Douglas is not at Nottingham. The boy at Manchester is not reading History; the boy at Nottingham is reading chemistry; Douglas is not reading Biology.

What subject is Tom reading, and where?

91 FOOTNOTE TO WISDEN

Among cricketers who made their county debut last year were Messrs. Glide, Cutt, Broomhandle, and Stonewall. All are amateurs. They earn their living (not necessarily respectively) as accountant, farmer, engineer, and poet, and the counties for which they play are (in alphabetical order) Domeshire, Holmshire, Loamshire, and Muddlesex.

Geoffrey Glide and the engineer are both spin bowlers. Blake Broomhandle keeps wicket for Muddlesex; the poet is a wicket keeper, too. Sam Stonewall scored a century against Loamshire. Charlie Cutt did even better against Holmshire, scoring 219 not out; playing against Loamshire, he stumped four of his opponents.

There is no farmer in the Muddlesex team.

What is the name of the engineer, and for which county does he play?

92 FOGTHEBOYS HALL

Fogtheboys Hall is, in its way, a competent private school, though it has not, so far, asked for periodical inspection by the Ministry of Education. The staff engaged by Dr. Knowall, the principal, consists entirely of ticket-of-leave men (whose services are relatively cheap) and for this reason they all function pseudonymously. They are known to the boys as Messrs. English, French, Latin, Greek, and Science.

Each of these five gentlemen teaches two of the subjects of which his colleagues are the namesakes. No master teaches the same two subjects, and each of the five subjects is taught by two masters.

For example, the namesakes of the two subjects taught by Mr. French both teach English, while the namesakes of the two subjects taught by Mr. English both teach Latin. No master teaches a subject of which the namesake teaches the subject corresponding to that master's name. Thus, if Mr. Greek teaches Latin, Mr. Latin does not teach Greek. Only one master—Mr. Science—is totally ignorant of Greek.

Which of the five masters teach science?

93 SIX LANGUAGES

At a recent international conference English was the principal language spoken, but interpreters were also present who could, if required, translate what was said into French, German, Dutch, Spanish, Arabic, and Turkish. Mr. Polyglot, of the Foreign Office, went to the trouble of engaging interpreters whose surnames corresponded to these six foreign tongues. Each of his six interpreters spoke two of the six foreign languages; no two of them spoke the same two languages; each of the six languages was spoken by just two of them. And none of them spoke the language of which he is the namesake.

Mr. Spanish, for example, could speak Dutch and German, while one of his colleagues (his brother-in-law) spoke Dutch and Arabic. Mr. French and Mr. Dutch, between them, spoke all four of the languages of which neither is the namesake. Of the two languages spoken by Mr. Dutch, both the namesakes spoke French.

Neither of the German-speaking interpreters had any knowledge of Arabic.

What two languages were offered by Mr. Turkish?

94 DEDICATEES

Nowadays no one writes a novel without dedicating it to someone. Each of five novelists whose works have recently appeared has dedicated his book to the only daughter of one of the others. No daughter is the recipient of more than one dedication.

Mr. Scarlet's novel is dedicated to Mr. White's daughter, Frances. Mr. White's novel is dedicated to Mary; Mr. Lemon's, to Anne; Mr. Green's, to Joan.

Mary is the daughter of the novelist who dedicated his book to Mr. Black's daughter.

Kate is Mr. Lemon's daughter.

Who is the father of her particular friend, Anne?

95 COLORFUL ISLES

Problems concerning the Colorful Isles will be familiar to you. The Blues, you will recall, invariably tell the truth. The Whites invariably lie. The Pinks tell the truth and lie alternately; but a Pink's first answer may be either truthful or otherwise.

Tom, George, Dick, and Harry—all natives of the Colorful Isles—are seated at a circular table enjoying a modest pint. George is on Tom's left, and Harry on Tom's right.

To them enters Jones, an inquisitive visitor. To each native in turn he puts these three questions (in the same order): (1) "What is the race to which your left-hand neighbor belongs?" (2) "And the chap sitting opposite to you?" (3) "And your right-hand neighbor?" Here are the answers which he receives:

Tom's answers: (1) Blue; (2) Pink; (3) Pink.
George's answers: (1) White; (2) Pink; (3) Pink.
Dick's answers: (1) White; (2) Blue; (3) Pink.
Harry's answers: (1) White; (2) Blue; (3) Pink.

To which race, in fact, does each of the four natives belong?

96 THE DRAGONFLIES

"Have you found out any more about these Dragonflies?" said Inspector Gimlett to his deputy.

"A little, Sir," said Sergeant Snipe. "There certainly is such an organization; but whether it's subversive or not I haven't so far discovered."

"Then what have you discovered?"

"That there's a lot of mumbo jumbo connected with it. I learned something from a bloke who was once a member. To communicate with the Head Dragonfly—or whatever the fellow's called—one had to begin by ringing up a phone number. The number was 0588, but my informant couldn't remember the exchange. Then one had to give, in succession to a series of questions, three other numbers: each of them of four digits. My bloke could only remember the last, which—he's sure of this—was 7647. At that time, by the way, they called themselves the Seventeenth International."

"They did, did they?" said Gimlett, who was doodling on his blotting pad.

"So he said. It seems pretty pointless to me."

"Pointless," murmured Gimlett. "Maybe you've got something there, Snipe."

What, presumably, were the other two numbers?

97 THE BIG-GAME HUNTERS

"We're having a thrilling time," writes Lady Blanche Hyena from M'Bongaland. "Big-game hunting. The party consists of Lalage Lion and her father, the Admiral; Mr. and Mrs. Gnothing Gnu; Lord Giraffe; and myself.

"Very appropriately, we've confined ourselves to shooting Lion, Gnu, Giraffe, and Hyena.

"Two competitions have been organized, in which so many

points each were given—in ascending order—for each Hyena, Giraffe, Gnu, and Lion added to the 'bag.' If one shot one of each, one scored 22 points. We adopted the same point-basis in both competitions.

"The results were remarkable. In the first competition all six of us bagged the same number of beasts; in the second competition I bagged one more than each of the others. In both competitions each of us scored 30 points. What is even more remarkable, the total of 30 was made up in twelve different ways. According to the Admiral, there are only fourteen ways in which it could have been arrived at.

"In the first competition, all four beasts were included in Mr. Gnu's bag. Lord Giraffe, on the other hand, had beasts of only one kind. Lalage bagged the largest number of Hyena, and I did better than anyone else in the Gnu department Mrs. Gnu, like myself, failed to bag a Lion.

"In the second competition, Lion bagged most Lion, and I most Giraffe. Gnu's beasts were all of one kind. Lalage and Lord Giraffe had a side-bet on Gnu, and she bagged two to his one."

What beasts were "bagged" by their own namesakes?

98 THE LATEST FROM LADY BLANCHE

Lady Blanche Hyena writes again from M'Bongaland:

"We are here for our annual big-game shoot. This year the party consists of last year's quartet—Rear-Admiral Lion, Lord Giraffe, Mr. Gnothing Gnu, and myself—with the addition of Mrs. Rhino. (How I detest that woman!) As usual, we are running the shoot on a competitive basis, giving one point or more for each beast shot. A rhino counts most points; then comes a lion; then a giraffe; then a gnu; then a hyena.

"Yesterday the party bagged eleven beasts, totaling thirty points. Everyone's namesake was represented in the bag. On the point basis, we were successful in the following order:

"(1) Mr. Gnu, (2) the Rhino woman, (3) Lord Giraffe, (4) me, (5) Rear-Admiral Lion. Yet Lion bagged twice as many beasts as anybody else. Gnu, I may tell you, scored points for a gnu, which some of the party think should have counted to me. A special prize was offered to anyone who could bag a pair of giraffes, but that no one succeeded in winning.

"Gnu is a solver (on and off) of those horrid Caliban problems. He tells me that if you 'gnu' our basis of scoring you could easily deduce who shot what. But Lion goes farther and says you could deduce our scoring basis, if I tell you that it only admits of one interpretation of the figures and facts I have given you."

What animals were shot by each member of the party?

99 MOULTING FEATHERS

Last summer I spent a week or so in the little-known village of Moulting Feathers, in Dumpshire. Its social center is the local Bird Fanciers' Club.

The Club has seven members. Each is the owner of one bird. And each owner is, strange to say, the namesake of the bird owned by one of the others.

Three of the fanciers have birds which are darker than their owners' feathered namesakes.

I stayed with the human namesake of Mr. Crow's bird, from whose wife I collected most of the village gossip. Incidentally, only two of the fanciers—Mr. Dove and Mr. Canary—are bachelors.

Mr. Gull's wife's sister's husband is the owner of the raven—the most popular of the seven birds. The crow, on the other hand, is much disliked; "I can't abide him," said his owner's fiancée.

Mr. Raven's bird's human namesake is the owner of the canary, while the parrot's owner's feathered namesake is owned by the human namesake of Mr. Crow's bird.

Who owns the starling?

100 TWO TABLES AT BRIDGE

At the Greens' family party, two tables sat down to play bridge. Those participating were Messrs. Green, Pink, Black, and White, and their respective wives.

White's partner was his daughter. Pink was playing against his mother. Black's partner was his sister. Mrs. Green was playing against her mother, Pink and his partner had the same mother. Green's partner was his mother-in-law.

No player's uncle was participating.

Who partnered whom? and how were the tables made up?

SOLUTIONS

1 CATS AMONG THE PIGEONS

Call the five fanciers D, H, Fd, Fo, and M. Call their wives' cats D/c, etc., and their favorite pigeons D/p, etc. Then we have the following scheme:

		FANCIERS	CATS	VICTIMS
1st clue	.	D	D/c	x/p
1st clue	.	x	x/c	M/p
2nd clue	.	H	H/c	D/p
3rd clue	.	y	y/c	Fo/p
3rd clue	.	Fd	Fd/c	y/p

—where x and y have to be identified with two of the symbols D, H, *etc.*

Now clearly x is not D, M, or H; and y is not D, H, Fd, or Fo. So y is M and it follows that x is Fd. We now have four of the five lines completed, and the fifth can only be Fo—Fo/c—H/p. **So Mr. Heath's pigeon was killed by Mrs. Forest's cat.**

2 INVOCATION

All the clues necessary to solve the problem are given.

The invocation is DUCDAME (*As You Like It*, II. 5: "An invocation to call fools into a circle."). This is obviously the right clue: it has seven letters, for the elimination of seven boys; and the first letter is D, which—proceeding clockwise on the "eeni-meeni-mo" principle—eliminates Boor.

The seven victims are selected in the following sequence:

D	count	4	Boor
U	„	21	Lollipop-Lollipop
C	„	3	Jay
D	„	4	Nosey

```
A  count   1  Stingo
M    „    13  Crayfish
E    „     5  Foolardy
```

So the boy who escapes flogging is Widdershins.

3 MR. YELLOW

A very simple puzzle!

Only a Lemon can say that he's not White; for a White, if he said so, would be lying; and an Orange would be telling the truth.

So Mr. White is the Lemon; and Mr. Lemon, who says he is not a Lemon, must be the White. Hence he tells the truth about Mr. Yellow.

Mr. Yellow is a White.

4 FIVE CANDIDATES

This is a quite simple inferential exercise. The data seem inadequate, but it will be found they are in fact just sufficient.

(1) The total marks must be 75. Ainsworth has 24, which leaves 51 for the other four candidates. Emerson, with the lowest mark, secures 5 for Greek and 3 for Philosophy; so his minimum is 11. It will be found that he cannot score more than this; the only possible totals are: Ainsworth 24; Borrow 15; Coleridge 13; Defoe 12; Emerson 11.

(2) Now set out the data in tabular form:

	ENG.	HIST.	LATIN	GREEK	PHIL.	TOTAL
AINSWORTH	5	5	5	4	5	24
BORROW						15
COLERIDGE	3	3	3	3	1	13
DEFOE						12
EMERSON	1	1	1	5	3	11

Defoe's marks must be 4 2 2 2 2, for all 5's and 3's are accounted for. And one of his 2's must be in Greek (since A has 4 already).

Hence Borrow scored 1 mark in Greek.

5 EXCHANGE OF AMENITIES

This is a rather difficult little puzzle. It is most readily tackled by setting out the data in tabular form:

DONOR	PRESENT	DONEE
HAM	SHERRY	PORT
WHISKY		
GOOSE		
SHERRY	n	
PORT		
	PORT	m
m	GOOSE	HAM
n		GOOSE
x		SHERRY

Here m and n are at present unknown, and we have to discover x.

Call Ham, Whisky, etc., H, W, and so on. If we could complete the table fully, H, W, G, S, P would each appear once in each column; and none twice in the same line.

Now m is clearly not P, G, or H. So m is S or W. But if m is S, n is G (for S sends n). This is impossible. It follows that m is W. And, since S sends n, and n sends to G, n can only be P. Now we can set out all the ascertainable facts:

DONOR	PRESENT	DONEE
HAM	SHERRY	PORT
WHISKY	GOOSE	HAM
GOOSE		SHERRY
SHERRY	PORT	WHISKY
PORT		GOOSE

Mr. Sherry's gift (either whisky or a ham) was presented by Mr. Goose.

6 ACCOMPLISHMENTS

This is quite a simple exercise. Call the girls M, L, A, V; their instruments *c*, *v*, *o*, *h*; their languages F, G, I, S. Then we have these possibilities:

M	*c*	FGS
L	*ov*	FIS
A	*ho*	FGI
V	*vh*	GIS

But the girl who plays the violin speaks French; this must be Lorna. Hence Anthea is the organist and speaks German. So only Mary can speak Spanish. **Valerie plays the harp and speaks Italian.**

7 YACHTS

Here are the data:

OWNER	DAUGHTER	YACHT
Spinnaker	—	*Iris*
Buoy	Iris	*Daffodil*
Luff	—	—
Gybe	—	*Anthea*
Windward	Lalage	*Jonquil*

Obviously, Mr. Luff's yacht is the *Lalage*. What is Mr. Luff's daughter's name? Clearly, not Iris or Lalage. Nor yet Daffodil, for Daffodil's father would then own the *Daffodil*; nor yet Jonquil, for Daffodil would then be Mr. Windward's daughter. So Mr. Luff's daughter is Anthea, and Mr. Gybe's daughter is Daffodil.

It follows that Jonquil's father is Mr. Spinnaker.

8 THE FACETIOUS FANCIERS

It is hardly necessary to reproduce in full the longish sequence of inferences, as this is a very simple problem. It will be found that the winners in the several classes were: **Guinea Pig,**

Mr. Cat; Duck, Mr. Canary; Cat, Mr. Pigeon; Rabbit,
Mr. Duck; Pigeon, Mr. Rabbit; Dog, Mr. Guinea Pig;
Canary, Mr. Dog.

9 THE FORTY-NINE CLUB

There is no "mathematical" principle involved. But it
should not be difficult to deduce the "relevant components"
of each code number:

	PROBE	CALICO	THWACKSTRAW	CALIBAN
(1) Number of letters in surname	5	6	11	7
(2) Ordinal total of letters ($A=1$, $B=2$, etc.) .	56	43	147	42
(3) Add . .	49	49	49	49
	110	98	207	(98)

My name was changed to KALIBAN because Calico was
already No. 98; **so my code number is 106.**

10 PLATYPUS

Sorting out the data, we get the following:

G dispatches	T to M
a ,,	*b* ,, P
b ,,	M ,, *c*
P ,,	*c* ,, *d*

Z G P T M must each appear in all three columns and in three
different rows. So *b* is Z and it follows that *c* is G. This gives us:

G dispatches	T to M
T or M ,,	Z ,, P
Z ,,	M ,, G
P ,,	G ,, T or Z
T or M ,,	P ,, T or Z

But the recipient of the Platypus doesn't send a Manatee. Hence it's T who sends Z to P, and

Sir Matthew Manatee sends a Platypus to Colonel Tiger.

11 A FESTIVE CHRISTMAS

The "catch" in this problem is that it does not state explicitly on how many evenings "re-grouping" took place. That has to be deduced from Mrs. Brown's remark that every combination of partners was exhausted. There are nine (not eight) possible groupings, i.e.:

HUSBAND	1	2	3	4	5	6	7	8	9
B	P	W	G	P	P	W	W	G	G
P	B	G	W	W	G	B	G	B	W
W	G	B	P	G	B	G	P	P	B
G	W	P	B	B	W	P	B	W	P

Now set out the data, relating each grouping to the schedule shown above:

EVENING:	1	2	3	4	5	6	7	8	9
PINK	G		B	W					
BROWN	P			P			W	G	W
WHITE			P				P		G
GREEN		P			W	?		P	
GROUPING	5	2	8	4	1	3	7	9	6

In the case of all except the second, fifth, and sixth evenings, the data enable the complete grouping to be deduced. Now we have left the three evenings where two couples "interchange." The nominations of Green's partners on two of these occasions enable us to deduce who was his partner on the third.

On the sixth evening Green's partner was Mrs. Brown.

12 CARNIVORES AT PLAY

Set out the data in the form of a skeleton table:

	LIONS	TIGERS	WOLVES	LEOPARDS	
LIONS	—	4	m	n	(1)
TIGERS	1	—	s	t	(2)
WOLVES	m	s	—	x	(3)
LEOPARDS	n	t	y	—	(4)

Ex hypothesi, y is greater than x.

We are given that $(4+m+n)$, $(1+s+t)$, $(m+s+x)$, and $(n+t+y)$ are in descending order of magnitude. So the sum of (1) and (2) exceeds the sum of (3) and (4) by 4 at least. Hence $5-(x+y)$ is at least 4.

So $(x+y)$ can only be 0 or 1; but y is greater than x, so y is 1 and x is 0.

Again, (1) exceeds (3) by at least 2, so $4-(s-n)$ is at least 2; which implies that $(s-n)$ is not greater than 2.

Similarly, from (2) and (4), $(s-n)$ is at least 2. So $(s-n)$ is 2.

The four totals are now seen to be $(4+m+n)$, $(3+n+t)$, $(2+m+n)$, and $(1+n+t)$, and it is at once seen that m must equal t.

We can now reconstruct our table:

	LIONS	TIGERS	WOLVES	LEOPARDS	GOALS FOR	GOALS AGAINST
LIONS	—	4	m	n	$4+m+n$	$1+m+n$
TIGERS	1	—	$(n+2)$	m	$3+m+n$	$6+m+n$
WOLVES	m	$(n+2)$	—	0	$2+m+n$	$3+m+n$
LEOPARDS	n	m	1	—	$1+m+n$	$m+n$

So the Leopards beat the Wolves by 1 goal to 0, and the smallest number of goals scored was against the Leopards.

13 BERRIES ISLAND

Denote the three tribes by *B*, *L*, and *R*. Now each guide has made four statements:

TRIBE OF:	OTHER GUIDE	1st THROWER	2nd THROWER	3rd THROWER
Statement of				
1st Guide	*L*	*B*	*L*	*R*
2nd Guide	*L*	*R*	*B*	*L*

If both Guides are *L*, their first statements (about each other) are true; but their next "true" statements (about the second thrower) are inconsistent. Hence one at least is not an *L*.

If one is a *B*, all his statements are true and all the statements of the other are untrue. But in that case the latter is an *L*, and two of his statements would be true. Hence neither is a *B* and one at least is an *R*.

It follows that the other cannot be an *L* (for an *R* always lies) and must therefore also be an *R*. We now know that all eight statements are untrue.

Both guides are Rasps; and the three Javelin Throwers are (in order) a Logan, a Rasp, and a Black.

14 CELIA'S SIMPLE CIPHER

This is a simple transliteration cipher; one useful clue is that Miss Padgham can hardly have been called anything but "Georgie Porgie." The message runs:

> "Georgie Porgie, pudding and pie,
> Is out of sorts and p'raps will die;
> And that is why her thankless job
> Is now discharged by Ginger Nob.
> —Ends."

15 MNEMONIC

One; Two; Three; Four; Five; Six; Seven . . .
So the next three letters are E N T.

16 TOURNAMENT

Fifteen rubbers in all are played. I need not set them out
in detail. It will be found that the numbers of rubbers won by
the several players are: E, 9; D, 8; A, 6; B, 6; C, 1.
So Exit heads the list with nine rubbers.

17 BEAUTY CONTEST

There are just four possible "partitions" of the votes: (a)
3 2 0 0, (b) 3 1 1 0, (c) 2 2 2 0, (d) 2 1 1 1. Clearly B's
is (d) and we can set out the framework of our voting table:

	Votes for			
	A	B	C	D
A:				
B:	1	2	1	1
C:			0	
D:				3

Now A gives the same vote to B and C; this cannot be 1, for
then C would get 3 votes from D. So A's line is 1 2 2 0 (c);
D's is 0 0 2 3 (a); and C's is 3 1 0 1 (b). The table is now
completed.

**Adela gets three votes from Colchicum; one from
Acorn; one from Blackbird.**

18 YACHTING GIRLS

This is a fairly simple "inferential." Set out the data in tabular form:

OWNER	DAUGHTER	YACHT
Collingwood	Thalia	*Lorna*
Drake	?	*Melissa*
Hood	Melissa	*Gabrielle*
Nelson	?	*Rosalind*
Benbow	?	?

Clearly Benbow's yacht is named *Thalia*. What is the name of Benbow's daughter? Not Gabrielle; for Gabrielle's father would then own the *Gabrielle*. Not Lorna, for Gabrielle would then be Collingwood's daughter.

So Benbow's daughter is Rosalind; and Nelson's daughter (owner of the *Rosalind*) is Gabrielle.

So Lorna is the daughter of Colonel Drake.

19 BRACELETS

Call the three colors R Y G.

The first point to bear in mind is that a bracelet can be looked at from either side. Thus the arrangement R R Y R G Y G becomes, when the bracelet is turned over, R R G Y G R Y.

Suppose a girl has selected 3R's, 2Y's, 2G's. How many bracelets can she construct? We will classify them with respect to the arrangement of the three R's.

(1) Arrangements R R R *x x x x*. There are four possibilities: *x x x x* can be G G Y Y; G Y Y G; Y G G Y; G Y G Y.

(2) Arrangement R R *x* R *x x x*. This is the only asymmetrical arrangement, and there are six possibilities. The *x / x x x* can be G / G Y Y; G / Y G Y; Y / Y G G; G /Y Y G; Y / G Y G; Y / G G Y.

(3) Arrangement R R *x x* R *x x*. There are four possibilities: G G / Y Y; G Y / G Y; G Y / Y G; Y G / G Y.

(4) Arrangement R x R x R x $\dot{x}$. Again there are four possibilities. They are G / G / Y Y; G / Y / G Y; G / Y / Y G; Y / Y / G G.

So there are 18 possibilities with 3R's; and, obviously, 18 each with 3G's and 3Y's: 54 in all.

It follows that there are 54 girls in the class.

20 A NOVEL CHAMPIONSHIP

G must have won against W and T. He can only have scored 3 points. So P scores 2 points, losing to T and W, which means that W beats T. The table is:

	G	P	W	T		Pts.
G . .	—	L	W	W	. .	3
P . .	W	—	L	L	. .	2
W . .	L	W	—	W	. .	2
T . .	L	W	L	—	. .	1

So Webbe lost to Granger, but won against Prickles and Tivey.

21 WONDERFUL

Each letter in the cipher represents another one. Transliteration would not be impossible without Peggy's additional clue; it might, however, take some time. But the added hint "too wonderful" should ring a bell with most solvers. The reference is to Proverbs 30 : 19: "The way of an eagle in the air," &c. The cipher, decoded, runs: **"The way of a man with a maid."**

22 UPPANDOWNE

(1) The answer "None of us is an Upwright" can only be given by a Downwright; it is therefore a lie and there must be at least one Upwright in the party.

(2) With one answer still to come there may be one, two, or three Upwrights. What answer from the sixth villager will solve the problem "beyond a peradventure"? Consider the several possibilities:

If the sixth villager says "Six," "Five," or "Four," there can only be one Upwright.

If he says "Three" there can be either one Upwright or three; if he says "Two" there can be either one or two.

If he says "None," there can only be one Upwright. He cannot answer "One."

So the answer given was "Six," "Five," "Four," or "None." In any case, **there was only one Upwright in the party.**

23 ALBERT'S UMBRELLA

The first essential is to set out the data intelligibly. If we call the diners by their initials, we have:

	HAT	GLOVES	UMBRELLA
A	k		
B	m		
C		n	
D			k
E			
m		C	
n			D
?	A		B
	D		not E

This table assembles what we know in a form in which the several facts can be correlated. For example, the relationships A . . . k and D . . . k remind us that Donald took the umbrella whose owner's hat was taken by Albert. The relationship D . . . not E reminds us that whoever took Donald's hat did not also take Edward's umbrella. And so on.

Any clue can be made the starting point of a series of related inferences. Suppose we start with A . . . *k* and D . . . *k*. The symbol *k* obviously stands for B, C, or E. Try each in turn, testing the conclusions which follow against those derived from other data. It will be found that *k* can only be C. And so on . . .

The unique solution which emerges is:

	HAT	GLOVES	UMBRELLA
A	C	D	E
B	E	A	D
C	D	B	A
D	B	E	C
E	A	C	B

So Charlie took Albert's umbrella.

24 BOOKS

(1) There are just five ways of allocating the books: (*a*) 4 0 0 0; (*b*) 3 1 0 0; (*c*) 2 2 0 0; (*d*) 2 1 1 0; (*e*) 1 1 1 1.

(2) Now set out the data diagrammatically. It will be found that the whole of the facts can be deduced:

	RECIPIENTS				
	A	B	C	D	E
Alice:	–	(1)	(1)	(1)	(1)
Bessie:	4	–	0	0	0
Cissie:	0	0	–	(1)	(3)
Deborah:	0	2	2	–	0
Edith:	0	(1)	(1)	(2)	0

So distribution (*a*) is Bessie's; (*e*) must be Alice's; (*b*) is Cissie's. Now Edith has four books, so distribution (*c*) is Deborah's. The rest follows.

Deborah received one book from Alice, one from Cissie, and two from Edith.

25 STAFF CONFERENCE

This puzzle is not as difficult as it may, at first blush, seem to be. Call the masters A, B, E, F, H, and their subjects *a, b, e, f, h.*

(1) A does not teach *a*; nor does he teach *e, f,* or *h,* since he attributes each of these subjects to someone else. So A teaches *b.*

(2) The English master is not E; nor A (teaching *b*); nor B; nor H. So F teaches *e.* And now we can deduce that E thinks F teaches *a.*

(3) We can also deduce that B teaches *f.* For A teaches *b,* and H erroneously thinks that *f* is taught by E.

(4) We have now sufficient data to compile a table showing facts and misattributions. Each letter must appear once in each rank and once in each column.

ATTRIBUTES TO

MASTER	A	F	H	B	E
A	*b*	*f*	*e*	*h*	*a*
F	*h̄*	*e*	*f*	*a*	*b*
H	*e*	*h̄*	*a*	*b*	*f*
B	*a*	*b*	*h̄*	*f̱*	*e*
E	*f*	*a*	*b*	*ē*	*ẖ*

The letters underlined show the subjects actually taught.
Hence the English master (Mr. French) thought the algebra master (Mr. History) taught French.

26 DRAKE GOES WEST

If each player plays three games against each of the others in his section, the number of games played must be found from:

Number in section	3	4	5	6	7	8
Number of games played	9	18	30	45	63	84

But 81 games are played in two sections. Hence there can only have been 4 players in one section and 7 in the other. **There were eleven competitors in all.**

27 BUNS

Eleven boys bought themselves 43 buns.
With buns at 2, 3, 4, and 6 cents each, 12 cents can be spent in exactly eleven ways:

66   633   642   6222   444   4422   4332   42222
3333   33222   222222

i.e., on 43 buns in all.
Each boy was allowed to spend 12 cents on himself.

28 BATTLE OF WITS

Mary's "generosity" is overrated. When John has scored 12 points, Mary should, at worst, have scored 3. Now they change over. Mary should score 18 points while John is scoring, at most, 7.
Mary should win by 2 points at least.

29 TEN STATELY TREES

This is very simple. Consider the first and third clues. These give us two possibilities:

PLANTER		TREES	
		I	II
Miss	A	BS	BS
,,	B		S
,,	F	S	
,,	O	AF	AB
,,	S		

Now consider the second clue. Given Scheme I, "Muffins" (Miss F) can plant S and O, and we get:

Miss A	BS
„ B	FO
„ F	SO
„ O	AF
„ S	AB

But the second clue will be found to be incompatible with Scheme II. So Scheme I is unique.

Belinda Beech planted one fir tree and one oak.

30 PICKLED WALNUTS

The clues are quite straightforward when one comes to sort them out.

(*i*) All armadillos can speak the Basque dialect (3), therefore (*ii*) all armadillos are eligible for the Tintinnabulum Club (5).

Therefore (*iii*) all armadillos prefer Mozart to Beethoven (7).

Therefore (*iv*) no armadillo ever takes a taxi in Bond Street (2).

Therefore (*v*) no armadillo carries a collapsible umbrella (9).

Therefore (*vi*) no armadillo can be registered as a philatelist (4).

Therefore (*vii*) no armadillo is ever invited to Professor Piltdown's parties (6).

Whence (1 and 8) we arrive at the conclusion: **no armadillo enjoys pickled walnuts.**

31 DIGITS ARE SYMBOLS

This is a simple sum. S E must be 25 or 36. A few moments' experiment will show that it cannot be 25, for there is no perfect square $2x5x$. So S E is 26, and S T E T is 3969, which is the square of 63.

Hence the sum of S E E and T E S S is the sum of 366 and 9633, i.e., 9999.

So the answer is T T T T.

32 ALLSPORTS

(1) The girl who is at Sandville is yachting. Amelia is not at Sandville, and yachting does not appeal to Celia, so Bella is yachting at Sandville.

(2) Celia is not at Mudville; it follows that Amelia is.

(3) So Celia is at Rockville, and hence is not playing golf.

Therefore Amelia is playing golf at Mudville.

33 PINK, WHITE, AND BLUE

(1) Mr. Pink is not the Blue; for if he were, he would say so.

(2) Mr. Pink is not the Pink. For if he is, his first answer is truthful. But if his first answer is truthful, his third answer is truthful also. Now, however, his second answer is likewise truthful; which is impossible.

(3) So Mr. Pink is the White. It follows that all his answers are untruthful. Mr. White is the Blue, and **Mr. Blue is the Pink.**

34 YACHTING AT NORMOUTH

With the aid of a framework we can set out the data:

OWNER	M	Y	G	N	C
Tues.		V			
Wed.			A		x
Thurs.	A	M	y	P	
Fri.	y	C			
Sat.			x		

Each of the letters representing a yacht (V A M P C) must appear once in each row and once in each column. The same letter must appear in the spaces *x x*; the same letter in *y y*. It is at once obvious that Yawl sailed *Porpoise* on Wednesday and *Atlantis* on Saturday, and that *y* represents *Vivandière*. Successive inferences will show that **Admiral Crabbe sailed, in succession, Porpoise, Mosquito, Candida, Atlantis, Vivandière.**

35 HOLIDAYS

Set out the data:

NAME	HOME	HOLIDAY
A		
B		D
C		*m*
D		
E	*m*	
n	B	E
m		B

m cannot be C, or E, or B, or D. So *m* is A.
Hence *n* is D.
So Mr. Exmouth is at Clacton.

36 POKER

This puzzle can only be solved by (intelligent) trial. Draw a plan of the table; start with any of the clues; then successively add data derived from the others.

It will be found that two arrangements are consistent with all the data. They are:

Mr. Baker
(farmer)

Mr. Farmer
(dyer)

Mr. Dyer
(hosier)

Mr. Glover
(baker)

Mr. Hosier
(glover)

AND:

Mr. Baker
(hosier)

Mr. Hosier
(glover)

Mr. Farmer
(dyer)

Mr. Dyer
(baker)

Mr. Glover
(farmer)

We cannot determine all five vocations, but we know that
Mr. Farmer is the dyer.

37 TWENTY MARBLES

You have to consider every possibility. If you draw 8
marbles, the stipulated conditions will probably be fulfilled,
but "probably" is not good enough. To draw 8 marbles may
leave all 8 blue ones, and only two of each of the other colors.
To draw 7, however, covers all contingencies.
Seven marbles should be drawn.

38 WHIST

Call the players B, D,A,S. Call their vocations *b*, *d*, *a*, *s*.
B is not *b*, nor is he *s* (his partner). So B is *a* or *d*.

If B is *a*, B (*a*) and A (*s*) sit opposite one another. But now *d* cannot be on S's right.

So the only possible arrangement of players is:

$$A(b)$$

$$D(s) \qquad\qquad B(d)$$

$$S(a)$$

Hence Mr. Banker (dentist) sat on the banker's left.

39 THREE ISLANDERS

(1) If the first native is a Blue, he must himself be Mr. Pink. But in that case the second native gives two truthful answers and must also be a Blue—which is impossible.

(2) By the same argument, the second native cannot be a Blue.

(3) So the third native is a Blue and must be Mr. Blue. His answers are truthful; hence:

Mr. Blue is a Blue; Mr. White is a Pink; and Mr. Pink is a White.

40 MIMULA

This is a puzzle which has long exercised the minds of mathematicians; and I believe I am right in saying that no completely rigorous proof of the answer has so far been put forward. But it is easy to demonstrate (by experiment) that **the maximum number of necessary colors is four,** i.e., it is impossible to draw on a plane surface a map on which more than four areas are contiguous.

41 MACBETH

Call the five "Thespians" B, Mb, Md, Du, and Db. Then the clues can be summarized as follows:

NAME	REHEARSED	PLAYED
B	s	
Mb		
Md	Db	B
Du		
Db	t	
s		Mb
t		Md

Now we must identify s and t. s cannot be B, or Db, or Mb, or Md; so s is Du. And t cannot be Db, or Du, or Md, or B (for if t is B, there is no one to rehearse Mb). Hence t is Mb. Now the table can be completed. Mb rehearses the part of B, finally played by Mr. Macduff.

So the answer is Mr. Macduff.

42 PIOUS CIRCLE

The "message" is a mnemonic. "Pious Circle" is the clue. Counting the number of letters in each word, and inserting a decimal point, we get:

$$3.14159265358$$

This is the value of "pi" (the relation of the circumference of a circle to its diameter) calculated to 11 places of decimals.

43 FALSEHOODS

One of the four quoted statements is true.

(1) Let the first statement be true. Then we have two hatters (Mr. D and Mr. B). So this hypothesis is out.

(2) Let the second statement be true. Then Mr. G is *d*; Mr. B is *h*; Mr. H is *b*. It follows that Mr. D is *g*.

(3) Let the third statement be true. Then Mr. H is *b*. So Mr. D is neither *b*, *h*, nor *d*, and, once again, must be *g*.

(4) Let the fourth statement be true. Now Mr. B is *h*. Mr. G is not *h*, *d*, or *g*, and so is *b*. Whence, as before, Mr. D is *g*.

Hence, while we cannot with certainty identify any of the others, we know that **Mr. Draper is the grocer.**

44 COMMENTATOR

Call the publicists A, B, C, D, E; call their pseudonyms A, J, M, P, T. Then construct the following scheme:

	A	B	C	D	E
Arnott	1	2	3	4	5
Brisk	J	6	M	7	8
Cellini	9	10	11	P	12
Dacres	M	P	13	14	15
Ewart	16	17	18	A	19

Each of the letters A, J, M, P, T must appear once in each column and once in each row. But since each writer knows his own pseudonym, 1, 6, 11, 14, and 19 must all be different.

7 must be T; 14, J; 4, M; 6, A; 8, P. 11 must be T (for J has been used for 14 and A for 6). And so on.

Arnott is "Prospero," Brisk is "Alba," Cellini is "Thunderer," Dacres is "Jove," Ewart is "Magnus."

45 POOTLE BEACH

A simple diagram solves this puzzle:

	T	F	N	C
Race 1	f			
Race 2		n	x	
Race 3				c
Race 4	x			

Let T F N C stand for the competitors; $t f n c$ for their yachts. Let x be *Firefly*. Then x is clearly neither f nor n, and cannot be c, for c is *Meteor*. So x is t. Now the table can be completed. *Meteor* is C's yacht; *Firefly* is T's; *Swallow* (sailed by C in the last race) is N's.

So *Vega* is owned by Mrs. Feeble.

46 CECILIA'S CODE

(1) One of the factors of E E E must be either 37 or 74.

(2) The following, therefore, are possible solutions of the question originally posed:

	A B	C D	E E E
(1)	37	12	444
(2)	37	18	666
(3)	37	24	888
(4)	74	12	888

or any of the above with the values of A B and C D reversed.

(3) Now test each of the above, in the light of Cecilia's second datum. This, it will be found, is only consistent with (1). So A B is 37; D is 2; and **their product in Cecilia's code is B E.**

47 MR. ETCHER

Call the artists D, E, M, S; their vocations, *d, e, m, s*. Then S must be *d* or *m*.

(1) If S is *d*, M is *s* or *e*. But, if M is *s*, *d* is the namesake of M's vocation.

So we have: S*d*; M*e*; E*s*; D*m* (for if E is *m*, the namesake of E's vocation is *e*).

(2) If S is *m*, M is *d*; for if M is *e*, E is *d* (impossible); and if M is *s*, E is *d* and D is *e* (impossible).

So we have: S*m*; M*d*; E*s*; D*e*.

Hence, collating (1) and (2), **Mr. Etcher can only be the sculptor.**

48 TELLHAM NUTHEN

(1) We can rule out at once the possibility that all three speakers are Washingtons.

(2) If they are all Longbows, the first speaker's comment would be true, which is impossible. Hence either there is one Washington or there are two Washingtons.

(3) If there are two Washingtons, the second speaker's remark is untrue, and the third speaker's is true, which is inconsistent with the data.

(4) Hence there is one Washington. What the second speaker says is true, and what the third says is false.

I.e., the third speaker is a Longbow.

49 SIX DINNERS

Call the four friends B, G, H, D.

There are, of course, just six ways in which they can be seated: in clockwise order, they are:

(1) B	G H D		(2) B	G D H	
(3) B	D G H		(4) B	D H G	
(5) B	H D G		(6) B	H G D	

Now we can quickly determine who is who.

Call the four vocations b, g, h, d. From the first and second clues, G is d. From the third clue, H is g. Whence (from the second clue) B is h; hence D is b.

So the seating arrangements were:

Monday:	B	G	H	D	(1) above
Tuesday:	B	D	G	H	(3) ,,
Wednesday:	B	H	D	G	(5) ,,
Thursday:	B	H	G	D	(6) ,,
Friday:	B	D	H	G	(4) ,,

This leaves (2), i.e., B G D H, for Saturday.

On Saturday, Mr. Hosier sat on Mr. Butcher's right, and Mr. Glover sat on Mr. Butcher's left.

50 PETS

Let A, B, C, D stand for the four relevant names.

Then we can present the data according to the following scheme:

Owner:	A	B	C	D	m	n	p
Dog:			p			A	
Cat:	m	p			n		C

We have to determine m, n, and p.

(1) p is either A or B. Let p be A. Then n is D, and m owns the cat D. Then m cannot be A (for A owns C), or B (for B would own B), or C (for C owns A), or D (for D would own D). Hence p is B. Now we have:

Owner:	A	B	C	D
Dog:	C	A	D	B
Cat:	D	C	B	A

So the dog David is owned by Cyril.

51 GREEN CROSSES

Call the candidates C, W, B.

C argues as follows: "Suppose my cross is red. Then W (or B) sees one green cross and one red cross. But W (like me) is a scholarship candidate and therefore intelligent. He will be saying: 'Suppose my cross is red. If it were, B would not have put his hand up, for he would be seeing two red crosses.' Hence, if mine is a red cross, W (or B) should by this time have deduced that his own cross is green. It follows that my cross is green also."

The above is the "logical" solution. But I think that it is equally commendable if Chuckles makes this answer: "The test, sir, would not be fair if two of us had green crosses and the third a red one."

52 CIPHER

"To be or not to be: That is the question."

Did you think of H A M L E T as the word which P R I N C E represents? If so, it should have given you a good start.

53 FOUR STATEMENTS

Of statements (2) and (4), one must be true. And, if (2) is true, either (1) or (4) must be true also.

So (4) is the true statement and the other three are false, **i.e., Mr. Driver is the guard; Mr. Fireman is the driver; Mr. Guard is the fireman.**

54 THREE NATIVES

Set out the three sets of answers so as to facilitate comparison, while preserving their order:

	GEORGE	EDWARD	WILLIAM	GEORGE	EDWARD
GEORGE		White	Pink	Blue	
EDWARD			Pink	Pink	Blue
WILLIAM	White	Blue	Blue		

Now a native's first and third answers are either both true or both false. If G's first and third answers are both true, G is Blue and E is White. But E agrees with G about William. So G's first and third answers are false.

If G's second answer is a lie, G is White. Then William's first answer, and also his third, are true. In this case William is Blue (impossible, as his answers do not agree with E's).

So G's second answer is true. **He is a Pink,** lying the first time. And now it is obvious that **William is also a Pink,** and also lying the first time, and that **Edward is a Blue.**

55 ZOO

Since the square of Z O O has only five digits, Z must be 1, 2, or 3.

But no square of an integer ends in 2 or 3; so Z is 1.

It follows that O is 9.

Hence T O P A Z is 39,601.

So T O P, in the same notation, is 396; P A T is 603.

And their sum, in Celia's notation, is OOO.

56 THREE HORSES

This isn't very difficult. Let A stand for Antrobus (etc.) and we have:

RIDER	HORSE	OWNER
N		A
W	N	
x	W	
D	x	

Since x is clearly A, the table becomes:

N	D	A
W	N	D
A	W	N
D	A	W

So Antrobus's horse is Daydream, and **Daydream rode the horse Antrobus.**

57 SCHOLARSHIP

Any statement can be made one's starting point. Thus, if one begins with Joan's statement, either Joan was fourth and Mollie was not second; or Mollie was second, and Joan was not fourth. Now, assume that Joan *was* fourth. It follows (from Pat's statement) that Edwina did better than Mollie. Test the relevant possibilities by the light of other statements. It will be found that they all fail, and hence Mollie was second. And so on.

It will be found that the only positional order consistent with the data is: (1) Pat; (2) Mollie; (3) Joan; (4) Edwina; (5) Gay.

58 TALLYHO

Call the six houses Q W H B L T:

Rounds:	Q	W	H	B	L	T
1	H	*a*	Q	*b*	*c*	*d*
2	W	Q	*e*	*f*	*g*	*h*
3	*i*	B	*j*	W	*k*	*l*
4	*m*	*n*	L	*o*	H	*p*
5	*q*	*r*	*s*	*t*	*u*	*v*

Each of the six letters must appear once in each row and once in each column. Moreover, where H appears in column Q, Q must appear in column H in the same round; and so on.

Now clearly j is T; so l is H. It follows that i is L and that k is Q. It follows that e is B and that s is W; and so on.

It will be found that on the fifth Saturday, Twickenham played Quorn.

59 NAMESAKES

Using initials (G B L T M) we have:

L represents G
T   ,, m
m ,, n
n ,,   L

Now n is not L (whom he represents); not T (for T, m, n are three people); nor G (for if so both T and G would represent L); not B (*ex hypothesi*). So n must be M. It follows that m is B.

So the poet Tennyson was represented by Joe Gladstone.

60 THREE VILLAGERS

(1) We can clearly rule out the possibility that all three were Washingtons.

(2) If there were two Washingtons, the first villager tells the truth, and the other two are lying; so that is impossible.

(3) If there is only one Washington, the first villager is lying, and the other two are telling the truth. So that is impossible, too.

It follows that **all three speakers were Longbows.**

61 EQUESTRIAN

This type of puzzle is confusing unless the data are carefully tabulated:

HORSE	OWNER	RIDER
	C	L
m	L	
	P	*m*
C	*n*	
P		*n*

Clearly *m* is either C or J and *n* is either J or L. But if *m* is J, *n* must be L, and now L owns two horses.

So *m* is C, and it is at once apparent that *n* is L. Now we have the complete table:

HORSE	OWNER	RIDER
P	C	L
C	L	J
J	P	C
L	J	P

So the rider of Lambkin was Pipkin, who owns the horse Jorkin.

62 AT RANDOM

This is strictly an "intelligence test."

(1) It is not necessary to calculate the number of marbles in the original bag. (The number is, in fact, six.) But, since there are equal numbers of blue marbles and of red ones, the odds against two blue marbles being drawn are equal to the odds against red marbles being drawn; i.e., 4 to 1.

(2) A *random* transference of some of the marbles to Bag No. 2 does not affect these odds. **It is still 4 to 1 against both marbles drawn being blue.**

63 DOMINANT FIFTH

The key is, of course, "Dominant Fifth." Take the fifth letter, then the fifth letter after that, and so on, canceling successive letters on the "Eeni-meeni-mini-mo" principle. The message is:

MEET IN THE CLASSROOM AT SEVEN.

64 "I'M A WASHINGTON"

Call a Washington W; a Longbow L.

The first speaker is obviously L, for if all four were Longbows none could say so.

Hence there is at least one W.

The second speaker must be L also; for if he is W, the third speaker is W too, and the third contradicts the second.

The third speaker may be W, in which case the fourth is W too; or he may be L, in which case the fourth is the only W.

I.e., the fourth speaker must be a Washington.

65 CASCA

Let A B C D F represent the five initials of both horsemen and horses. Then we have:

HORSEMAN	TRAINED	RODE
A	m	n
B		p
C		m
D	n	
F		
n		D
p		B

n is clearly B, C or F. But it will be found that, if n is B, D as well as A rides B. Similarly, n cannot be C. So n is F.

It follows that A trains B and rides F; that B rides C; that C rides B; and that D trains F.

So Casca was trained by Fox.

66 BUSES

This is purely an "intelligence test." Most of the data are red herrings. Since each bus plies continuously backwards and forwards, and there are eleven in all, **Mr. Brightly passed ten.**

67 BOREHAM

Working backwards from the boy's age, the several dates can be calculated at sight:

Boreham's son was born on June 13, 1936.
Boreham was born on May 13, 1892.
Boreham's father was born on April 13, 1849.
Boreham's grandfather was born on March 13, 1806.
Boreham's great-grandfather was born on February 13, 1764.

And his great-great-grandfather was born on January 13, 1722.

68 CONFERENCE

Call the six languages (and interpreters) F G S D P W.

Consider the first three clues: that Mr. F and Mr. D speak (between them) G S P W; that, of the languages spoken by Mr. D, both the namesakes speak F; and that Mr. S speaks D and G. There are three possibilities:

	I		*II*		*III*	
Mr. F	G	S	S	W	S	P
Mr. G			F		F	
Mr. S	D	G	D	G	D	G
Mr. D	W	P	G	P	G	W
Mr. P	F		F			
Mr. W	F				F	

But *II* is ruled out by the fact that no one speaks G P, and *III* by the fact that someone speaks D P, and this cannot be Mr. P. Hence *I* is unique. Mr. G speaks D P; Mr. W speaks F S, and **Mr. Polish speaks French and Welsh.**

69 TRANSLITERATE

Did you notice that the last eight letters were the same as the first eight? The message (very appropriate, I thought) is:

ONCE MORE UNTO THE BREACH, DEAR FRIENDS, ONCE MORE.

70 PENNY GREEN

It's quite simple, really. After each Penny Green train, there's an interval of (say) three minutes before a Shillingstone train comes in. In which case, the next Penny Green train appears after an interval of a quarter of an hour.

71 CROSS CURRENTS

Dolores Dizzy was agent for Mr. Pussyfoot; and Pussyfoot was not the Socialist candidate, nor was Miss Dizzy the Communist agent. It follows that Pussyfoot and Miss Dizzy were, respectively, the Liberal candidate and agent.

Next, we know that the Socialist candidate was Dizzy, and that the Communist agent was Miss Fabian; since the Communist candidate's daughter was the Socialist agent, these can only have been Mr. and Miss Gladstone. And now it is obvious that the Tory candidate was Mr. Marx, and his daughter the Total Abstainer's agent, and that **the Total Abstainer was Mr. Fabian.**

72 A FAIR COP

If X X multiplied by X X produces M M C C, X X can only be 88.

M M C C is 7744.

So we have to find the square of 22, i.e., 484.

Which, in Cecilia's code, is C X C.

73 SLITELY FONEY

Tabulating the data, we have:

NAME	1ST	2ND	3RD
A		n	
E			
F		t	
G	m		
S			
m	E	S	
n	G	F	
t	A		E

It follows that m is A or F; n is E or S; and t is G or S. Very little trial will give a unique solution:

NAME	1ST	2ND	3RD
A	S	E	F
E	G	F	A
F	E	S	G
G	F	A	S
S	A	G	E

So the French prizes went (1) to German; (2) to English; (3) to Algebra.

74 MISS BRIGHTSANDS

The five votes can be "partitioned" in seven ways: (*a*) 5-0-0-0-0; (*b*) 4-1-0-0-0; (*c*) 3-2-0-0-0; (*d*) 3-1-1-0-0; (*e*) 2-2-1-0-0; (*f*) 2-1-1-1-0; (*g*) 1-1-1-1-1.

We can easily allot the partitions to those who adopted them. G's is (*a*); H's is (*b*); J's is (*f*) (Susan getting two votes); D's is (*g*). So C's must be (*d*); B's is (*e*); and therefore A's is (*c*). Now, with the aid of two or three straightforward inferences, the voting table can be completed:

		E	L	D	M	S
GIRLS						
G	(*a*)	5	.	.	.	.
H	(*b*)	.	4	.	.	1
J	(*f*)	1	1	.	1	2
D	(*g*)	1	1	1	1	1
C	(*d*)	.	.	1	1	3
B	(*e*)	.	1	2	2	.
A	(*c*)	.	.	3	2	.

So Susan's votes were: three from Cyril; two from John; one from Harry; one from Dick. Alec gave three votes to Diana and two votes to Mary.

75 SANDRA

This is an old friend in a new setting. The Cormorant is herself Sandra's mother.

76 SURNAMES

If we consider the first two clues, it is obvious that W's sons must be TG, TJ, or GJ; and that J's sons must be TF, TW, or FW. Testing each of the first three pairs in combination with each of the second three, three possibilities emerge:

FATHER	SONS		
	1	2	3
T	FG	FG	WJ
G	FJ	WJ	FT
F	WJ	GW	GT
W	TG	TJ	GJ
J	TW	TF	FW

But neither of F's sons is a W, which rules out 1 and 2.
So Mr. Thomas's boys are named James and Walter.

77 NUMBER PLATES

Take the "digital total" of each car: i.e., add its component digits; if the total is over 9, add again:

SAM	2075	$2+0+7+5 = 14$	$1+4 = 5$
HEN	8862	$8+8+6+2 = 24$	$2+4 = 6$
EDW	4534	$4+5+3+4 = 16$	$1+6 = 7$
ROY	6183	$6+1+8+3 = 18$	$1+8 = 9$

Now, the surnames Jones, Carter, Butcher, Patterson contain (respectively) 5, 6, 7, and 9 letters.
So Roy's car was EDW 4534.

78 NINE DANCES

Set out first the nine ways (there are just nine) in which the eight dancers can be paired:

		HUSBAND			
		A	B	C	D
WIVES:	1	B	A	D	C
	2	C	D	A	B
	3	D	C	B	A
	4	B	C	D	A
	5	B	D	A	C
	6	C	A	D	B
	7	C	D	B	A
	8	D	A	B	C
	9	D	C	A	B

Now, the 4th, 5th, and 6th dances must have been arrangements 2, 5, 7. It follows that the first three dances were 1, 4, 6. This leaves 3, 8, 9, which represent the 7th, 8th, and 9th dances.

So, for the last dance, Alibi's partner was Mrs. Dunce; Boron's, Mrs. Camomile; Camomile's, Mrs. Alibi; and Dunce's, Mrs. Boron.

79 THE RUMPUS CLUB

All that one needs to solve this puzzle is a clear head and the capacity to draw diagrams. Any of the six statements made to Daubwell can be taken as one's starting point. Alternative diagrams of the table should be drawn, embodying possible arrangements, and rejected as soon as the data from the next clue considered produce an impossible result. Considerations of some eight or nine diagrams will give the unique solution.

The seating at the table (in clockwise order) was: (**1**) **Lord Crocus (Egbert)**; (**2**) **Lord Rumple (Albert)**; (**3**) **Lord Rumple's brother (Herbert)**; (**4**) **Lord Crocus's cousin (Ethelbert)**; (**5**) **Lord Rumple's cousin (Gilbert)**; (**6**) **Lord Crocus's brother (Robert)**.

80 REGATTA

Admiral White is not sailing *White*, *Brown*, or *Green*, so he must be sailing *Moon*. So the yacht *Brown* will be sailed neither by Admiral White nor by Dr. Moon; i.e., it will be sailed by Captain Green. The owner of *Moon* is not Dr. Moon; nor Captain Green; nor Admiral White, who is sailing her. So *Moon* is owned by Mr Brown.

Admiral White does not own *Moon*, *Green*, or *White*, so he must be the owner of *Brown*. It follows that Dr. Moon owns *Green*, and that Captain Green owns *White*. *Green* cannot be sailed by Dr. Moon, her owner; she is therefore sailed by Mr. Brown.

It follows that **Captain Green's yacht *White* will be sailed by Dr. Moon.**

81 EPICENE

Represent the four names by A, H, J, and S.

(1) Who is A's brother? Not A, nor J (her fiancé); i.e., A's brother is either S or H.

(2) Let S be A's brother. Then the girl J (engaged to H) must be A's sister; H is J's sister; S is H's sister. This is impossible, for H (the son) would be playing in both sets of tennis. So the brother of A is H; of H, J; of J, S; and of S, A.

(3) Turning now to the parents, the girl A's father must be J; for, if he is S, J's (the son's) father is A. This is impossible, as two parents would be playing in both Canasta games.

Here then is the completed table of relationships:

FATHER	MOTHER	SON	DAUGHTER
J	S	H	A
S	A	J	H
A	H	S	J
H	J	A	S

So Jocelyn's husband is Hilary.

82 CISSIE'S PARTY

Six girls can be seated around a table in 120 different ways; but there is no need to draw 120 diagrams—or, indeed, any diagrams at all.

(1) Consider B's statement. If this is true both A and D are lying. But F's statement contradicts both C's and E's; so if B is telling the truth there are three liars at least.

(2) By a similar process of reasoning, F must be the second liar. Hence the statements of A, B, D, and E are true. In cyclic order, the girls are seated: **Cissie; Betty; Doris; Antoinette; Frances; Evelyn.**

83 MIXED DOUBLES

Call the four men G P B W; call their wives *g p b w*.

There are nine possible ways in which the eight players can be paired to provide two matches in an evening:

		1	2	3	4	5	6	7	8	9
G	partners	*p*	*b*	*w*	*p*	*p*	*b*	*b*	*w*	*w*
P	,,	*g*	*w*	*b*	*b*	*w*	*w*	*g*	*b*	*g*
B	,,	*w*	*g*	*p*	*w*	*g*	*p*	*w*	*g*	*p*
W	,,	*b*	*p*	*g*	*g*	*b*	*g*	*p*	*p*	*b*

Each of the first three pairings produces matches for three evenings.

(1)   G *p*   *vs.*   P *g*;   B *w*   *vs.*   W *b*
(2)   G *p*   ,,   W *b*;   B *w*   ,,   P *g*
(3)   G *p*   ,,   B *w*;   W *b*   ,,   P *g*

But—here is the catch—each of the other six pairings only gives two evenings' matches. The third pair of matches will have been covered already.

So the tournament will occupy 21 evenings in all.

84 CROSSING THE BAR

Jimmy's message is confined to six letters. Is his key word the transliteration of a poet's name? The clue "Crossing the Bar" suggests Tennyson. Jimmy's further clue ("The key word ought to be obvious") is designed to lead to PASS KEYS, which is an exact transliteration. The message runs:

NO TEENY SONNETS YET? NONE, NOSEY; SO NO TOYS.—SONNY.

85 SIMPLE CIPHER

The "simplest possible type" of cipher is one in which one letter is substituted for another. It can only be solved, of course, by trial. Taking the "message" plus the two clues, there are eight S's; seven A's; five T's. These, one may presume, are three of the commoner letters (E T A I O S H). Try T O E for S A T, and the message begins:

TO.EO..OTTO.E

which is surely suggestive.

The cipher, in short, reads: TO BE OR NOT TO BE, THAT IS THE QUESTION. The first additional clue gives HAMLET and the second SOLILOQUY.

86 IMPERFECT MEMORIES

An inspection of the data shows that there must be at least three statements which are untrue. For (a) both R and P say that they sat South; (b) R's second statement and B's second statement contradict one another; (c) so do the second statements of W and P.

Hence the number of untrue statements is anything from three to eight.

The most straightforward approach is to set out diagrammatically the 24 ways in which the players can have been seated. It will be found that in only one case are as many as five statements true. Given any smaller number of true statements, there are alternative possibilities.

The three untrue statements are B's second one and both of P's.

And the seating of the players was: **South, Colonel Ratbane; East, Mrs. Beetle; North, Dr. Whatknott; West, Mrs. Peewit.**

87 MUSICAL FLOP

A simple enough puzzle if the data are set out intelligently. Call the four musicians B, C, M, Q, and their instruments p, c, f, o.

Then we have:

		B	C	M	Q
ASSIGNS TO	B	—			x
	C		—		p
	M	x	f	—	
	Q			c	—

In each row, and in each column, all three attributions must be different; but those in each column must be the same as those which figure in the corresponding row.

What, then, is x? It must be either c or o. But if x is o, the table cannot be completed. The unique solution is:

NAMES AND INSTRUMENTS

	B	C	M	Q
	o	c	p	f
B	—	p	f	c
C	f	—	o	p
M	c	f	—	o
Q	p	o	c	—

So Breve, who is the organist, took Crotchet to be the flutist.

88 SEVENTEEN MARBLES

The color distribution can be:

(a)	8	4	3	2
(b)	7	5	3	2
(c)	6	5	4	2

But to ensure that at least two of one color and at least one of a second color are drawn, the numbers which it is necessary to draw differ. In case (*a*), 12 must be drawn; in case (*b*), eleven; in case (*c*), ten. Hence the actual distribution is (*b*), and there are seven green marbles.

So to make sure of drawing at least one green marble, it is again necessary to draw eleven.

89 INTERHOUSE HOCKEY

Successive inferences show (1) that 10 goals were scored in each of the six games; (2) that the several scores were therefore 10–0, 9–1, 8–2, 7–3, 6–4, 5–5; (3) that the points scored must have been: D, 5; G, 4; N, 2; B, 1; (4) that D drew with B 5–5; (5) that N defeated B 10–0; (6) that D's two wins were 8–2 and 6–4.

The following table is therefore as follows:–

	D	G	N	B	PTS.	GOALS
D	—	8	6	5	5	19—11
G	2	—	9	7	4	18—12
N	4	1	—	10	2	15—15
B	5	3	0	—	1	8—22

Darling defeated Nightingale by six goals to four.

90 PROSPECTIVE GRADUATES

Douglas is not at Nottingham. So he is either at Manchester or at Reading.

But since he is not at Nottingham, he is not reading Chemistry nor is he reading Biology.

He is therefore reading History, and so cannot be at Manchester, i.e., he is at Reading.

It follows that John is at Nottingham and is reading Chemistry.

So Tom is reading Biology at Manchester.

91 FOOTNOTE TO WISDEN

This problem, though the clues are designed to confuse, is a very simple "inferential." Starting with any clue, and eliminating successive alternatives, we get this unique solution:

NAME	PROFESSION	COUNTY
Glide	Farmer	Loamshire
Cutt	Poet	Domeshire
Broomhandle	Accountant	Muddlesex
Stonewall	Engineer	Holmshire

So Sam Stonewall is the engineer, and he plays for Holmshire.

92 FOGTHEBOYS HALL

Call the masters (and subjects) E, F, L, G, S.

From the first clue, the subjects taught by F are G S, L S, or L G. Consider each of these in turn.

(1) If F teaches G S, G and S teach E, and L and E teach F. So F teaches L, which is impossible, since F already teaches G S.

(2) If F teaches L S, L and S teach E, and G and E teach F. It now follows that L teaches S, G teaches L, and E and S teach G. But this is impossible, since S knows no G.

(3) So F teaches L G and the only solution consistent with all the data is:

F : LG	L : EG
G : ES	E : SF
S : FL	

So the two masters who teach science are Mr. Greek and Mr. English.

93 SIX LANGUAGES

This is a simple enough problem. Call the six languages
A D F G S T. Then Mr. S. speaks D G, and Mr. D and Mr. F
speak between them A G S T. There are six possibilities, but
three are excluded at once by the fact that Mr. D cannot
speak S, for Mr. S does not speak F. Hence:

(1) Mr. D speaks G T, and Mr. F speaks A S. This would
mean that Mr. G and Mr. T speak F, leaving Mr. A to speak
A D, which is impossible.

(2) Mr. D speaks A G and Mr. F speaks S T. But this is
impossible because (last clue) no one speaks A G. Hence

(3) Mr. D speaks A T and Mr. F speaks G S. This gives us a
unique solution. Mr. G speaks A D; Mr. A speaks F T; and
Mr. Turkish offers French and Spanish.

94 DEDICATEES

(1) Obviously Black's novel is dedicated to Kate, since the
other four are all accounted for.

(2) Black's daughter is the "dedicatee" of the novel written
by Mary's father. Who, then, is Black's daughter? Not Frances;
not Kate; not Mary. Nor yet Anne, to whom Kate's father's
novel is dedicated.

(3) So Black's daughter is Joan, and Green is Mary's
father.
It follows that Anne's father is Mr. Scarlet.

95 COLORFUL ISLES

Whether a native is Blue, White, or Pink, his first and
third answers are either both true or they are both false.
Tabulate the several answers, so that they can be compared,
and underline the first and third. We have:

		TOM	· GEORGE	DICK	HARRY
Tom	.	—	B	P	P
George	.	P	—	W	P
Dick	.	B	P	—	W
Harry	.	W	B	P	—

There are several ways of attacking the problem. Here is one which is probably as simple as any:

(1) D says that T is B. If T is B, G is B. But D says that G is P. It follows that D's second statement is untrue, so D is either P or W.

(2) If D is P, T is B and H is W. But H says that T is B. It follows that D is W.

(3) So G is not P. Nor is G W, for he tells the truth about D. Hence G is B, and his answers tell us what we want to know.

Tom is a Pink (telling the truth the first time); George is a Blue; Dick is a White; Harry is a Pink (lying the first time).

96 THE DRAGONFLIES

There are two clues to this seemingly cryptic puzzle: "Seventeenth" and "pointless." One-seventeenth, expressed as a recurring decimal, is .0588 2352 9411 7647.

So it is a reasonable presumption that the other two numbers were 2352 and 9411.

97 THE BIG-GAME HUNTERS

Anyone can solve this problem, since it calls for no technical knowledge whatever; on the other hand, the solution demands care and patience.

First, we have to find four different numbers which total 22, and from which 30 can be built up in exactly 14 different ways. A little experiment will show that if 1 or 2 is included, the total number of available combinations is bound to exceed 14. There then fall for consideration these partitions of 22, which must be considered more carefully:

(1) 3 4 5 10   (2) 3 4 6 9   (3) 3 4 7 8   (4) 3 5 6 8
(5) 4 5 6 7

Trial will show that the last, and only the last, of these partitions gives 14 combinations totaling 30. All the others give more.

That 4, 5, 6, 7 is the right partition is confirmed by the fact that it yields 7 combinations of 6 elements and 5 of 5 elements. Here is the complete table.

Number	1	2	3	4	5	6	7	8	9	10	11	12	13	14
4 (Hyena) .	6	5	4	3	3	2	2	1	1	1				
5 (Giraffe) .		2			1	2	3	4	1		6	2	1	
6 (Gnu) .	1			3	1	2		1		2		1	3	5
7 (Lion) .			2		1		1		3	2		2	1	
Beasts .	7	7	6	6	6	6	6	6	5	5	6	5	5	5

The rest is simple. In the first competition, each competitor must have bagged six beasts. We have to consider, therefore, Nos. 3–8 and 11. Clearly Giraffe's bag is No. 11 and Gnu's is No. 5. Lalage's is No. 3 and Lady Blanche Hyena's is No. 4. Mrs. Gnu's might have been No. 6 or No. 8, but consideration of the data regarding the second competition shows that No. 8 was Lady Blanche's second "bag." So Mrs. Gnu's is No. 6 and Admiral Lion's is No. 7.

Turning now to the second competition, we know that No. 8 is Lady Blanche's "bag." Lion's is No. 9; Gnu's is No. 14; Lalage's is No. 10; Giraffe's is No. 12. This leaves No. 13 for Mrs. Gnu.

Hence the "beasts 'bagged' by their own namesakes" are:

FIRST COMPETITION

Admiral Lion:	**1 Lion**
Lalage:	**2 Lion**
Mr. Gnothing Gnu:	**1 Gnu**
Mrs. Gnothing Gnu:	**2 Gnu**
Lord Giraffe:	**6 Giraffe**
Lady B. Hyena:	**3 Hyena**

SECOND COMPETITION

Admiral Lion:	**3 Lion**
Lalage:	**2 Lion**
Mr. Gnothing Gnu:	**5 Gnu**
Mrs. Gnothing Gnu:	**3 Gnu**
Lord Giraffe:	**2 Giraffe**
Lady B. Hyena:	**1 Hyena**

98 THE LATEST FROM LADY BLANCHE

(1) It is at once clear that points were scored as follows:

$$
\begin{aligned}
\text{Mr. Gnu} &= 8 \\
\text{Mrs. Rhino} &= 7 \\
\text{Lord Giraffe} &= 6 \\
\text{Lady Blanche} &= 5 \\
\text{Rear-Admiral Lion} &= 4
\end{aligned}
$$

(2) Also it is obvious that Lion scored for 4 beasts (hyena) at 1 point each.

This leaves 7 beasts that collectively yielded 26 points, distributed 2, 2, 2, 1 (for Lion shot twice as many as anybody else). It is clear also that no beast scores 8, as Gnu's bag (8 points) includes a gnu or giraffe.

(3) Now consider the possible distribution of the individual scores:

$$
\begin{aligned}
8 &= 7+1 \text{ or } 6+2 \text{ or } 5+3 \text{ or } 4+4 \\
7 &= 7 \quad\; \text{ or } 6+1 \text{ or } 5+2 \text{ or } 4+3 \\
6 &= 6 \quad\; \text{ or } 5+1 \text{ or } 4+2 \text{ or } 3+3 \\
5 &= 5 \quad\; \text{ or } 4+1 \text{ or } 3+2
\end{aligned}
$$

(4) If $8 = 4+4$, 4 is the value of a gnu and the others must be greater. This would mean that two shot one beast only. Hence a gnu scores 2 or 3.

Hence the following scale of points must be considered for beasts other than hyenas:

Gn.	Gi.	L.	R.
2	3	4	5
2	3	4	6
2	3	4	7
2	3	5	6
2	3	5	7
2	3	6	7*
2	4	5	6
2	4	5	7*
2	4	6	7*
2	5	6	7†
3	4	5	7
3	4	6	7*
3	5	6	7*

Of these the distribution † yields no solution, and all except those marked * yield more solutions than one.

Analyzing these five distributions:

No.	Gn.	Gi.	L.	R.	8	7	6	5
1	2	3	6	7	6+2	7	3+3	3+2
2	2	4	5	7	7+1	5+2	4+2	5
3	2	4	6	7	6+2	7	4+2	4+1
4	3	4	6	7	7+1	4+3	6	4+1
5	3	5	6	7	7+1	6+1	3+3	5

But only (1) and (3) of the above are admissible, since only these distributions give Gnu points for a gnu, and (1) is ruled out by the fact that Giraffe bags a pair of giraffes.

Hence the point basis is 1, 2, 4, 6, 7 and

> **Mr. Gnu bags a lion and a gnu.**
> **Mrs. Rhino bags a rhino.**
> **Lord Giraffe bags a giraffe and a gnu.**
> **Lady Blanche bags a giraffe and a hyena.**
> **Rear-Admiral Lion bags 4 hyenas.**

99 MOULTING FEATHERS

(1) The raven's owner's feathered namesake must be a light-colored bird. Hence the raven is owned by one of the following: Mr. Dove, Mr. Canary, Mr. Gull, Mr. Parrot. The first two of these are bachelors and the raven is owned by Mr. Gull's wife's sister's husband—i.e., **Mr. Parrot owns the raven.**

(2) Mr. Crow owns a light-colored bird, but Mr. Crow's bird's human namesake is married. Hence Mr. Crow owns either the parrot or the gull. But Mr. Crow cannot own the parrot, for the parrot's owner's feathered namesake is owned by the human namesake of Mr. Crow's bird; and Mr. Parrot, we know, owns the raven. Therefore **Mr. Crow owns the gull.**

(3) Mr. Raven must own the parrot, the gull, or the dove. But Mr. Crow owns the gull, and if Mr. Raven owns the parrot two people would own the raven. Whence **Mr. Raven owns the dove** and

(4) **Mr. Dove owns the canary.**

(5) The crow's owner is unmarried; hence **Mr. Canary owns the crow.** Whence:

(6) **Mr. Starling owns the parrot** and

(7) **Mr. Gull owns the starling.**

100 TWO TABLES AT BRIDGE

(1) White's partner was his daughter—i.e., Mrs. Green, Mrs. Pink, or Mrs. Black.

> (a) Let White's daughter be Mrs. Green. Then they must be playing against Green and Mrs. White.

Then at the other table Black's partner is his sister, Mrs. Pink, who therefore is Pink's mother. This is impossible; so White's daughter is not Mrs. Green.

(*b*) Let White's daughter be Mrs. Pink. Then Green's partner is Mrs. Black or Mrs. White.

> (i) Let Green's partner be Mrs. White. Then Black's partner is Mrs. Green, and Pink's partner is Mrs. Black.
>
>> Then (I) if Mrs. Green and Mrs. Black are playing against one another, each is the other's mother.
>>
>> (II) if Mrs. Black and Mrs. Pink are playing against one another, Pink's wife is also his mother.
>>
>> (III) if Mrs. Black and Mrs. White are playing against one another, Pink and his wife have the same mother.
>
> So Green's partner cannot be Mrs. White.
>
> (ii) Let Green's partner be Mrs. Black. Then Pink's partner is Mrs. Green or Mrs. White.
>
>> (I) Let Pink's partner be Mrs. Green. Then Black's partner must be Mrs. White. Not possible as no player's uncle was participating.
>>
>> (II) Let Pink's partner be Mrs. White. Not possible, as Mrs. Pink would have married her mother's brother.
>
> So White's daughter cannot be Mrs. Pink.

(*c*) **Therefore White's daughter (and partner) is Mrs. Black.**

(2) Black's sister (and partner) cannot be Mrs. White (*supra*) and therefore is either Mrs. Pink or Mrs. Green.

    (*a*) Let Black's partner be Mrs. Green. Then Green's partner is Mrs. Pink.

        Then (i) Mrs. Pink is Pink's mother.

        or (ii) Mrs. White is the mother of both Mr. and Mrs. Black.

        or (iii) Mrs. White is her own daughter's daughter.

    (*b*) **It follows that Black's partner is Mrs. Pink.**

(3) **Also Green's partner is Mrs. White, and Pink's partner is Mrs. Green.**

This is how the eight players are seated:

White		**Pink**	
Black	**Mrs. Pink**	**Green**	**Mrs. White**
	Mrs. Black		**Mrs. Green**

A CATALOGUE OF SELECTED DOVER BOOKS
IN ALL FIELDS OF INTEREST

A CATALOGUE OF SELECTED DOVER BOOKS
IN ALL FIELDS OF INTEREST

AMERICA'S OLD MASTERS, James T. Flexner. Four men emerged unexpectedly from provincial 18th century America to leadership in European art: Benjamin West, J. S. Copley, C. R. Peale, Gilbert Stuart. Brilliant coverage of lives and contributions. Revised, 1967 edition. 69 plates. 365pp. of text.

21806-6 Paperbound $3.00

FIRST FLOWERS OF OUR WILDERNESS: AMERICAN PAINTING, THE COLONIAL PERIOD, James T. Flexner. Painters, and regional painting traditions from earliest Colonial times up to the emergence of Copley, West and Peale Sr., Foster, Gustavus Hesselius, Feke, John Smibert and many anonymous painters in the primitive manner. Engaging presentation, with 162 illustrations. xxii + 368pp.

22180-6 Paperbound $3.50

THE LIGHT OF DISTANT SKIES: AMERICAN PAINTING, 1760-1835, James T. Flexner. The great generation of early American painters goes to Europe to learn and to teach: West, Copley, Gilbert Stuart and others. Allston, Trumbull, Morse; also contemporary American painters—primitives, derivatives, academics—who remained in America. 102 illustrations. xiii + 306pp. 22179-2 Paperbound $3.00

A HISTORY OF THE RISE AND PROGRESS OF THE ARTS OF DESIGN IN THE UNITED STATES, William Dunlap. Much the richest mine of information on early American painters, sculptors, architects, engravers, miniaturists, etc. The only source of information for scores of artists, the major primary source for many others. Unabridged reprint of rare original 1834 edition, with new introduction by James T. Flexner, and 394 new illustrations. Edited by Rita Weiss. 6⅝ x 9⅝.

21695-0, 21696-9, 21697-7 Three volumes, Paperbound $13.50

EPOCHS OF CHINESE AND JAPANESE ART, Ernest F. Fenollosa. From primitive Chinese art to the 20th century, thorough history, explanation of every important art period and form, including Japanese woodcuts; main stress on China and Japan, but Tibet, Korea also included. Still unexcelled for its detailed, rich coverage of cultural background, aesthetic elements, diffusion studies, particularly of the historical period. 2nd, 1913 edition. 242 illustrations. lii + 439pp. of text.

20364-6, 20365-4 Two volumes, Paperbound $6.00

THE GENTLE ART OF MAKING ENEMIES, James A. M. Whistler. Greatest wit of his day deflates Oscar Wilde, Ruskin, Swinburne; strikes back at inane critics, exhibitions, art journalism; aesthetics of impressionist revolution in most striking form. Highly readable classic by great painter. Reproduction of edition designed by Whistler. Introduction by Alfred Werner. xxxvi + 334pp.

21875-9 Paperbound $2.50

THE ARCHITECTURE OF COUNTRY HOUSES, Andrew J. Downing. Together with Vaux's *Villas and Cottages* this is the basic book for Hudson River Gothic architecture of the middle Victorian period. Full, sound discussions of general aspects of housing, architecture, style, decoration, furnishing, together with scores of detailed house plans, illustrations of specific buildings, accompanied by full text. Perhaps the most influential single American architectural book. 1850 edition. Introduction by J. Stewart Johnson. 321 figures, 34 architectural designs. xvi + 560pp.

22003-6 Paperbound $4.00

LOST EXAMPLES OF COLONIAL ARCHITECTURE, John Mead Howells. Full-page photographs of buildings that have disappeared or been so altered as to be denatured, including many designed by major early American architects. 245 plates. xvii + 248pp. 7⅞ x 10¾.

21143-6 Paperbound $3.50

DOMESTIC ARCHITECTURE OF THE AMERICAN COLONIES AND OF THE EARLY REPUBLIC, Fiske Kimball. Foremost architect and restorer of Williamsburg and Monticello covers nearly 200 homes between 1620-1825. Architectural details, construction, style features, special fixtures, floor plans, etc. Generally considered finest work in its area. 219 illustrations of houses, doorways, windows, capital mantels. xx + 314pp. 7⅞ x 10¾.

21743-4 Paperbound $4.00

EARLY AMERICAN ROOMS: 1650-1858, edited by Russell Hawes Kettell. Tour of 12 rooms, each representative of a different era in American history and each furnished, decorated, designed and occupied in the style of the era. 72 plans and elevations, 8-page color section, etc., show fabrics, wall papers, arrangements, etc. Full descriptive text. xvii + 200pp. of text. 8⅜ x 11¼.

21633-0 Paperbound $5.00

THE FITZWILLIAM VIRGINAL BOOK, edited by J. Fuller Maitland and W. B. Squire. Full modern printing of famous early 17th-century ms. volume of 300 works by Morley, Byrd, Bull, Gibbons, etc. For piano or other modern keyboard instrument; easy to read format. xxxvi + 938pp. 8⅜ x 11.

21068-5, 21069-3 Two volumes, Paperbound $10.00

KEYBOARD MUSIC, Johann Sebastian Bach. Bach Gesellschaft edition. A rich selection of Bach's masterpieces for the harpsichord: the six English Suites, six French Suites, the six Partitas (Clavierübung part I), the Goldberg Variations (Clavierübung part IV), the fifteen Two-Part Inventions and the fifteen Three-Part Sinfonias. Clearly reproduced on large sheets with ample margins; eminently playable. vi + 312pp. 8⅛ x 11.

22360-4 Paperbound $5.00

THE MUSIC OF BACH: AN INTRODUCTION, Charles Sanford Terry. A fine, nontechnical introduction to Bach's music, both instrumental and vocal. Covers organ music, chamber music, passion music, other types. Analyzes themes, developments, innovations. x + 114pp.

21075-8 Paperbound $1.25

BEETHOVEN AND HIS NINE SYMPHONIES, Sir George Grove. Noted British musicologist provides best history, analysis, commentary on symphonies. Very thorough, rigorously accurate; necessary to both advanced student and amateur music lover. 436 musical passages. vii + 407 pp.

20334-4 Paperbound $2.75

THE PHILOSOPHY OF THE UPANISHADS, Paul Deussen. Clear, detailed statement of upanishadic system of thought, generally considered among best available. History of these works, full exposition of system emergent from them, parallel concepts in the West. Translated by A. S. Geden. xiv + 429pp.

21616-0 Paperbound $3.00

LANGUAGE, TRUTH AND LOGIC, Alfred J. Ayer. Famous, remarkably clear introduction to the Vienna and Cambridge schools of Logical Positivism; function of philosophy, elimination of metaphysical thought, nature of analysis, similar topics. "Wish I had written it myself," Bertrand Russell. 2nd, 1946 edition. 160pp.

20010-8 Paperbound $1.35

THE GUIDE FOR THE PERPLEXED, Moses Maimonides. Great classic of medieval Judaism, major attempt to reconcile revealed religion (Pentateuch, commentaries) and Aristotelian philosophy. Enormously important in all Western thought. Unabridged Friedländer translation. 50-page introduction. lix + 414pp.

(USO) 20351-4 Paperbound $2.50

OCCULT AND SUPERNATURAL PHENOMENA, D. H. Rawcliffe. Full, serious study of the most persistent delusions of mankind: crystal gazing, mediumistic trance, stigmata, lycanthropy, fire walking, dowsing, telepathy, ghosts, ESP, etc., and their relation to common forms of abnormal psychology. Formerly *Illusions and Delusions of the Supernatural and the Occult.* iii + 551pp. 20503-7 Paperbound $3.50

THE EGYPTIAN BOOK OF THE DEAD: THE PAPYRUS OF ANI, E. A. Wallis Budge. Full hieroglyphic text, interlinear transliteration of sounds, word for word translation, then smooth, connected translation; Theban recension. Basic work in Ancient Egyptian civilization; now even more significant than ever for historical importance, dilation of consciousness, etc. clvi + 377pp: 6½ x 9¼.

21866-X Paperbound $3.95

PSYCHOLOGY OF MUSIC, Carl E. Seashore. Basic, thorough survey of everything known about psychology of music up to 1940's; essential reading for psychologists, musicologists. Physical acoustics; auditory apparatus; relationship of physical sound to perceived sound; role of the mind in sorting, altering, suppressing, creating sound sensations; musical learning, testing for ability, absolute pitch, other topics. Records of Caruso, Menuhin analyzed. 88 figures. xix + 408pp.

21851-1 Paperbound $2.75

THE I CHING (THE BOOK OF CHANGES), translated by James Legge. Complete translated text plus appendices by Confucius, of perhaps the most penetrating divination book ever compiled. Indispensable to all study of early Oriental civilizations. 3 plates. xxiii + 448pp. 21062-6 Paperbound $3.00

THE UPANISHADS, translated by Max Müller. Twelve classical upanishads: Chandogya, Kena, Aitareya, Kaushitaki, Isa, Katha, Mundaka, Taittiriyaka, Brhadaranyaka, Svetasvatara, Prasna, Maitriyana. 160-page introduction, analysis by Prof. Müller. Total of 826pp. 20398-0, 20399-9 Two volumes, Paperbound $5.00

JOHANN SEBASTIAN BACH, Philipp Spitta. One of the great classics of musicology, this definitive analysis of Bach's music (and life) has never been surpassed. Lucid, nontechnical analyses of hundreds of pieces (30 pages devoted to St. Matthew Passion, 26 to B Minor Mass). Also includes major analysis of 18th-century music. 450 musical examples. 40-page musical supplement. Total of xx + 1799pp.
(EUK) 22278-0, 22279-9 Two volumes, Clothbound $15.00

MOZART AND HIS PIANO CONCERTOS, Cuthbert Girdlestone. The only full-length study of an important area of Mozart's creativity. Provides detailed analyses of all 23 concertos, traces inspirational sources. 417 musical examples. Second edition. 509pp.
(USO) 21271-8 Paperbound $3.50

THE PERFECT WAGNERITE: A COMMENTARY ON THE NIBLUNG'S RING, George Bernard Shaw. Brilliant and still relevant criticism in remarkable essays on Wagner's Ring cycle, Shaw's ideas on political and social ideology behind the plots, role of Leitmotifs, vocal requisites, etc. Prefaces. xxi + 136pp.
21707-8 Paperbound $1.50

DON GIOVANNI, W. A. Mozart. Complete libretto, modern English translation; biographies of composer and librettist; accounts of early performances and critical reaction. Lavishly illustrated. All the material you need to understand and appreciate this great work. Dover Opera Guide and Libretto Series; translated and introduced by Ellen Bleiler. 92 illustrations. 209pp.
21134-7 Paperbound $1.50

HIGH FIDELITY SYSTEMS: A LAYMAN'S GUIDE, Roy F. Allison. All the basic information you need for setting up your own audio system: high fidelity and stereo record players, tape records, F.M. Connections, adjusting tone arm, cartridge, checking needle alignment, positioning speakers, phasing speakers, adjusting hums, trouble-shooting, maintenance, and similar topics. Enlarged 1965 edition. More than 50 charts, diagrams, photos. iv + 91pp.   21514-8 Paperbound $1.25

REPRODUCTION OF SOUND, Edgar Villchur. Thorough coverage for laymen of high fidelity systems, reproducing systems in general, needles, amplifiers, preamps, loudspeakers, feedback, explaining physical background. "A rare talent for making technicalities vividly comprehensible," R. Darrell, *High Fidelity*. 69 figures. iv + 92pp.   21515-6 Paperbound $1.00

HEAR ME TALKIN' TO YA: THE STORY OF JAZZ AS TOLD BY THE MEN WHO MADE IT, Nat Shapiro and Nat Hentoff. Louis Armstrong, Fats Waller, Jo Jones, Clarence Williams, Billy Holiday, Duke Ellington, Jelly Roll Morton and dozens of other jazz greats tell how it was in Chicago's South Side, New Orleans, depression Harlem and the modern West Coast as jazz was born and grew. xvi + 429pp.
21726-4 Paperbound $2.50

FABLES OF AESOP, translated by Sir Roger L'Estrange. A reproduction of the very rare 1931 Paris edition; a selection of the most interesting fables, together with 50 imaginative drawings by Alexander Calder. v + 128pp. 6½x9¼.
21780-9 Paperbound $1.25

"ESSENTIAL GRAMMAR" SERIES

All you really need to know about modern, colloquial grammar. Many educational shortcuts help you learn faster, understand better. Detailed cognate lists teach you to recognize similarities between English and foreign words and roots—make learning vocabulary easy and interesting. Excellent for independent study or as a supplement to record courses.

ESSENTIAL FRENCH GRAMMAR, Seymour Resnick. 2500-item cognate list. 159pp.
(EBE) 20419-7 Paperbound $1.25

ESSENTIAL GERMAN GRAMMAR, Guy Stern and Everett F. Bleiler. Unusual shortcuts on noun declension, word order, compound verbs. 124pp.
(EBE) 20422-7 Paperbound $1.25

ESSENTIAL ITALIAN GRAMMAR, Olga Ragusa. 111pp.
(EBE) 20779-X Paperbound $1.25

ESSENTIAL JAPANESE GRAMMAR, Everett F. Bleiler. In Romaji transcription; no characters needed. Japanese grammar is regular and simple. 156pp.
21027-8 Paperbound $1.25

ESSENTIAL PORTUGUESE GRAMMAR, Alexander da R. Prista. vi + 114pp.
21650-0 Paperbound $1.35

ESSENTIAL SPANISH GRAMMAR, Seymour Resnick. 2500 word cognate list. 115pp.
(EBE) 20780-3 Paperbound $1.25

ESSENTIAL ENGLISH GRAMMAR, Philip Gucker. Combines best features of modern, functional and traditional approaches. For refresher, class use, home study. x + 177pp.
21649-7 Paperbound $1.35

A PHRASE AND SENTENCE DICTIONARY OF SPOKEN SPANISH. Prepared for U. S. War Department by U. S. linguists. As above, unit is idiom, phrase or sentence rather than word. English-Spanish and Spanish-English sections contain modern equivalents of over 18,000 sentences. Introduction and appendix as above. iv + 513pp.
20495-2 Paperbound $2.75

A PHRASE AND SENTENCE DICTIONARY OF SPOKEN RUSSIAN. Dictionary prepared for U. S. War Department by U. S. linguists. Basic unit is not the word, but the idiom, phrase or sentence. English-Russian and Russian-English sections contain modern equivalents for over 30,000 phrases. Grammatical introduction covers phonetics, writing, syntax. Appendix of word lists for food, numbers, geographical names, etc. vi + 573 pp. 6⅛ x 9¼.
20496-0 Paperbound $4.00

CONVERSATIONAL CHINESE FOR BEGINNERS, Morris Swadesh. Phonetic system, beginner's course in Pai Hua Mandarin Chinese covering most important, most useful speech patterns. Emphasis on modern colloquial usage. Formerly *Chinese in Your Pocket*. xvi + 158pp.
21123-1 Paperbound $1.75

ALPHABETS AND ORNAMENTS, Ernst Lehner. Well-known pictorial source for decorative alphabets, script examples, cartouches, frames, decorative title pages, calligraphic initials, borders, similar material. 14th to 19th century, mostly European. Useful in almost any graphic arts designing, varied styles. 750 illustrations. 256pp. 7 x 10.   21905-4 Paperbound $4.00

PAINTING: A CREATIVE APPROACH, Norman Colquhoun. For the beginner simple guide provides an instructive approach to painting: major stumbling blocks for beginner; overcoming them, technical points; paints and pigments; oil painting; watercolor and other media and color. New section on "plastic" paints. Glossary. Formerly *Paint Your Own Pictures.* 221pp.   22000-1 Paperbound $1.75

THE ENJOYMENT AND USE OF COLOR, Walter Sargent. Explanation of the relations between colors themselves and between colors in nature and art, including hundreds of little-known facts about color values, intensities, effects of high and low illumination, complementary colors. Many practical hints for painters, references to great masters. 7 color plates, 29 illustrations. x + 274pp.
20944-X Paperbound $2.75

THE NOTEBOOKS OF LEONARDO DA VINCI, compiled and edited by Jean Paul Richter. 1566 extracts from original manuscripts reveal the full range of Leonardo's versatile genius: all his writings on painting, sculpture, architecture, anatomy, astronomy, geography, topography, physiology, mining, music, etc., in both Italian and English, with 186 plates of manuscript pages and more than 500 additional drawings. Includes studies for the Last Supper, the lost Sforza monument, and other works. Total of xlvii + 866pp. 7⅞ x 10¾.
22572-0, 22573-9 Two volumes, Paperbound $10.00

MONTGOMERY WARD CATALOGUE OF 1895. Tea gowns, yards of flannel and pillow-case lace, stereoscopes, books of gospel hymns, the New Improved Singer Sewing Machine, side saddles, milk skimmers, straight-edged razors, high-button shoes, spittoons, and on and on . . . listing some 25,000 items, practically all illustrated. Essential to the shoppers of the 1890's, it is our truest record of the spirit of the period. Unaltered reprint of Issue No. 57, Spring and Summer 1895. Introduction by Boris Emmet. Innumerable illustrations. xiii + 624pp. 8½ x 11⅝.
22377-9 Paperbound $6.95

THE CRYSTAL PALACE EXHIBITION ILLUSTRATED CATALOGUE (LONDON, 1851). One of the wonders of the modern world—the Crystal Palace Exhibition in which all the nations of the civilized world exhibited their achievements in the arts and sciences—presented in an equally important illustrated catalogue. More than 1700 items pictured with accompanying text—ceramics, textiles, cast-iron work, carpets, pianos, sleds, razors, wall-papers, billiard tables, beehives, silverware and hundreds of other artifacts—represent the focal point of Victorian culture in the Western World. Probably the largest collection of Victorian decorative art ever assembled—indispensable for antiquarians and designers. Unabridged republication of the Art-Journal Catalogue of the Great Exhibition of 1851, with all terminal essays. New introduction by John Gloag, F.S.A. xxxiv + 426pp. 9 x 12.
22503-8 Paperbound $4.50

LAST AND FIRST MEN AND STAR MAKER, TWO SCIENCE FICTION NOVELS, Olaf Stapledon. Greatest future histories in science fiction. In the first, human intelligence is the "hero," through strange paths of evolution, interplanetary invasions, incredible technologies, near extinctions and reemergences. Star Maker describes the quest of a band of star rovers for intelligence itself, through time and space: weird inhuman civilizations, crustacean minds, symbiotic worlds, etc. Complete, unabridged. v + 438pp. 21962-3 Paperbound $2.50

THREE PROPHETIC NOVELS, H. G. WELLS. Stages of a consistently planned future for mankind. *When the Sleeper Wakes,* and *A Story of the Days to Come,* anticipate *Brave New World* and *1984,* in the 21st Century; *The Time Machine,* only complete version in print, shows farther future and the end of mankind. All show Wells's greatest gifts as storyteller and novelist. Edited by E. F. Bleiler. x + 335pp. (USO) 20605-X Paperbound $2.50

THE DEVIL'S DICTIONARY, Ambrose Bierce. America's own Oscar Wilde—Ambrose Bierce—offers his barbed iconoclastic wisdom in over 1,000 definitions hailed by H. L. Mencken as "some of the most gorgeous witticisms in the English language." 145pp. 20487-1 Paperbound $1.25

MAX AND MORITZ, Wilhelm Busch. Great children's classic, father of comic strip, of two bad boys, Max and Moritz. Also Ker and Plunk (Plisch und Plumm), Cat and Mouse, Deceitful Henry, Ice-Peter, The Boy and the Pipe, and five other pieces. Original German, with English translation. Edited by H. Arthur Klein; translations by various hands and H. Arthur Klein. vi + 216pp. 20181-3 Paperbound $2.00

PIGS IS PIGS AND OTHER FAVORITES, Ellis Parker Butler. The title story is one of the best humor short stories, as Mike Flannery obfuscates biology and English. Also included, That Pup of Murchison's, The Great American Pie Company, and Perkins of Portland. 14 illustrations. v + 109pp. 21532-6 Paperbound $1.25

THE PETERKIN PAPERS, Lucretia P. Hale. It takes genius to be as stupidly mad as the Peterkins, as they decide to become wise, celebrate the "Fourth," keep a cow, and otherwise strain the resources of the Lady from Philadelphia. Basic book of American humor. 153 illustrations. 219pp. 20794-3 Paperbound $1.50

PERRAULT'S FAIRY TALES, translated by A. E. Johnson and S. R. Littlewood, with 34 full-page illustrations by Gustave Doré. All the original Perrault stories—Cinderella, Sleeping Beauty, Bluebeard, Little Red Riding Hood, Puss in Boots, Tom Thumb, etc.—with their witty verse morals and the magnificent illustrations of Doré. One of the five or six great books of European fairy tales. viii + 117pp. 8⅛ x 11. 22311-6 Paperbound $2.00

OLD HUNGARIAN FAIRY TALES, Baroness Orczy. Favorites translated and adapted by author of the *Scarlet Pimpernel.* Eight fairy tales include "The Suitors of Princess Fire-Fly," "The Twin Hunchbacks," "Mr. Cuttlefish's Love Story," and "The Enchanted Cat." This little volume of magic and adventure will captivate children as it has for generations. 90 drawings by Montagu Barstow. 96pp. (USO) 22293-4 Paperbound $1.95

MATHEMATICAL PUZZLES FOR BEGINNERS AND ENTHUSIASTS, Geoffrey Mott-Smith. 189 puzzles from easy to difficult—involving arithmetic, logic, algebra, properties of digits, probability, etc.—for enjoyment and mental stimulus. Explanation of mathematical principles behind the puzzles. 135 illustrations. viii + 248pp.
20198-8 Paperbound $1.75

PAPER FOLDING FOR BEGINNERS, William D. Murray and Francis J. Rigney. Easiest book on the market, clearest instructions on making interesting, beautiful origami. Sail boats, cups, roosters, frogs that move legs, bonbon boxes, standing birds, etc. 40 projects; more than 275 diagrams and photographs. 94pp.
20713-7 Paperbound $1.00

TRICKS AND GAMES ON THE POOL TABLE, Fred Herrmann. 79 tricks and games— some solitaires, some for two or more players, some competitive games—to entertain you between formal games. Mystifying shots and throws, unusual caroms, tricks involving such props as cork, coins, a hat, etc. Formerly *Fun on the Pool Table.* 77 figures. 95pp.
21814-7 Paperbound $1.00

HAND SHADOWS TO BE THROWN UPON THE WALL: A SERIES OF NOVEL AND AMUSING FIGURES FORMED BY THE HAND, Henry Bursill. Delightful picturebook from great-grandfather's day shows how to make 18 different hand shadows: a bird that flies, duck that quacks, dog that wags his tail, camel, goose, deer, boy, turtle, etc. Only book of its sort. vi + 33pp. 6½ x 9¼. 21779-5 Paperbound $1.00

WHITTLING AND WOODCARVING, E. J. Tangerman. 18th printing of best book on market. "If you can cut a potato you can carve" toys and puzzles, chains, chessmen, caricatures, masks, frames, woodcut blocks, surface patterns, much more. Information on tools, woods, techniques. Also goes into serious wood sculpture from Middle Ages to present, East and West. 464 photos, figures. x + 293pp.
20965-2 Paperbound $2.00

HISTORY OF PHILOSOPHY, Julián Marias. Possibly the clearest, most easily followed, best planned, most useful one-volume history of philosophy on the market; neither skimpy nor overfull. Full details on system of every major philosopher and dozens of less important thinkers from pre-Socratics up to Existentialism and later. Strong on many European figures usually omitted. Has gone through dozens of editions in Europe. 1966 edition, translated by Stanley Appelbaum and Clarence Strowbridge. xviii + 505pp. 21739-6 Paperbound $3.00

YOGA: A SCIENTIFIC EVALUATION, Kovoor T. Behanan. Scientific but non-technical study of physiological results of yoga exercises; done under auspices of Yale U. Relations to Indian thought, to psychoanalysis, etc. 16 photos. xxiii + 270pp.
20505-3 Paperbound $2.50